Celebrity Catchmasters

T0098302

Simone Heng

Lee Wei Song

Benny Ong

Nancy Lam

Khoo Swee Chiow

Sir Stamford
Raffles

Ong Kim Seng

Suchen
Christine Lim

Chandran Nair

Ho Yeow Sun

THE GREAT
SINGAPORE QUIZ

monsoon

monsoonbooks

Published in 2008
by Monsoon Books Pte Ltd
52 Telok Blangah Road
#03-05 Telok Blangah House
Singapore 098829
www.monsoonbooks.com.sg

ISBN: 978-981-05-9210-3

Cover photograph copyright © iStockPhoto

Printed in Singapore

12 11 10 09 08   1 2 3 4 5 6 7 8 9

Introduction

Let the games begin.

Welcome to *The Great Singapore Quiz*, a handy yet substantial compendium brimming with a multitude of fascinating and thought-provoking questions to test your grey matter—however you choose to play.

On every page you'll find a quiz of ten questions, each on a different subject. Enough for a challenge and ideal for a 'round' if you want to make the quiz longer.

Each quiz has one question from the following ten categories: Arts and Literature, Food and Drink, Geography, Pop Culture, Sport, History, General Knowledge, Nature, Money and Power and Language. If you prefer to concentrate on questions from one particular category, you can easily pick them out of each quiz.

All questions relate to Singapore so you always have a chance to answer about the place you know and love the best.

Throughout the book we have the pleasure of presenting ten celebrity questioners. They'll each be bringing you a quiz and you can score extra with a special 'bonus' question about them or their activity.

You'll find all the answers in a separate section at the back of the book—so there is no danger of accidentally seeing them while you read the questions.

Quizzing Suggestions

The Great Singapore Quiz is highly versatile—there is no end to the ways in which you can use it:

Go Solo

No need for anyone else to ask the questions—why not do some 'mental push-ups' with a quiz on the journey to work or during your lunch break? Or keep your quiz book handy to pass the time whenever you're stuck in a queue.

One on One

Do you have a healthy rivalry with a friend? Test whose brain is best by doing the same quiz together. There's always another quiz if the result is a tie.

Family

The Great Singapore Quiz provides an ideal opportunity for some family fun. And it is perfect for getting everyone involved too. You can have one quizmaster with everybody answering individually, or you could divide into teams—girls vs. boys, old vs. young, wife's family vs. husband's family—and challenge each other.

Friends

Quizzes are a fantastic social activity. Whether the venue is a coffee shop, park, barbecue or bar, a great quiz will always get the discussion flowing, sparking laughter and building friendships.

It's just as important to exercise your mind as it is your body so go on, have a go, enjoy yourself and build up those mental muscles at the same time.

Quiz 1

Arts and Literature: Which Singapore theatre company staged *Confessions of Three Unmarried Women* (1987), *Block Sale* (1996) and *How Do You Know You're Chinese?* (1998)?

Food and Drink: Which company brews Tiger Beer?

Geography: Which former hotel, one of the three top hotels in Singapore in the early twentieth century, sat on the corner of Coleman Street and North Bridge Road?

Pop Culture: Which was the first cinema in Singapore to screen 'talkies' (films with dialogue) in the early 1930s?

Sport: In which sport did Abdul Halim Haron win an Asian Games gold medal despite holding down two jobs as a motorcycle despatch rider and part-time bouncer?

History: In which World War II battle in Singapore did Lieutenant Adnan Saidi die a war hero?

General Knowledge: Which mosque, located in Dunlop Street, has a large yellow and green sundial design on the front?

Nature: Which carnivorous plant drowns and dissolves its victims in a special liquid contained in its cup-shaped leaves?

Money and Power: Name the first prime minister of Malaysia.

Language: What does the acronym ASEAN stand for?

Quiz 2

Arts and Literature: Which Tamil theatre group has a name meaning 'Theatre of Fire'?

Food and Drink: What part of the plant does tapioca come from?

Geography: Which Indonesian resort island is just 20 km away from Singapore?

Pop Culture: Which black-and-white Malay comedy film, produced by Shaw Brothers, starred P. Ramlee, Aziz Sattar and S. Shamsuddin and was a big hit in 1957?

Sport: Which game, of Malay origin, involves moving counters or seeds around holes on a long board in order to collect them in a larger hole at either end of the board?

History: What were the Abingdon Tunnels used for during World War II?

General Knowledge: What are the 5 Cs every Singaporean is supposed to aspire to?

Nature: What is the only Singaporean island on which Red Junglefowl can be found?

Money and Power: Who has been Speaker of Parliament since 2002?

Language: In 1966 which language policy was introduced into Singapore's education system?

Quiz 3

Arts and Literature: In what year did Esplanade – Theatres on the Bay open?

Food and Drink: When frying crabs for dishes such as chilli crab, what colour should the shells turn when properly cooked?

Geography: How long is the Singapore River?

Pop Culture: What scantily clad entertainment was a popular draw at the Neptune Theatre Restaurant?

Sport: Which pool player won medals at six consecutive Southeast Asian Games from 1991 to 2001?

History: What was the name of the Japanese military police, much feared during the Occupation?

General Knowledge: What is the name of the mosque on South Bridge Road which has octagonal minarets?

Nature: What is the head of a monkey troop called?

Money and Power: What do Singapore Airlines, SingTel and DBS Bank have in common?

Language: 'Oh, mother!' can be expressed in Singlish in what way?

Quiz 4

Arts and Literature: Which accomplished Singaporean actor and director once starred with Anthony Hopkins in the London West End production of *M Butterfly*?

Food and Drink: What method of cooking involves simmering meat or vegetables in very little liquid for a specific period so that a distinctive flavour is produced?

Geography: What neighbouring geographical feature has been moved more than one kilometre away from Tanjong Katong since the 1950s?

Pop Culture: In the television sitcom *Phua Chu Kang*, what is the name of the main character's brother?

Sport: Which tenpin bowler amassed seven Southeast Asian Games gold medals between 1987 and 1995?

History: Whose visit to Singapore in 1968 provoked demonstrations and protests in neighbouring Malaysia, Indonesia and Brunei?

General Knowledge: Which Orchard Road building suffered a bomb blast on 10 March 1965?

Nature: What dangerous activity takes place at Nee Soon Swamp Forest?

Money and Power: What is the top personal income tax rate for Year of Assessment (YA) 2007?

Language: Which language do approximately 65% of Singapore's Indian community speak?

Quiz 5

Arts and Literature: Ivan Heng founded which theatre group in 2000?

Food and Drink: *Babi assam* is a dish created by braising diced belly pork in a liquid predominantly flavoured with which ingredient?

Geography: Which university can be found to the west of Jurong West new town?

Pop Culture: What is the nickname of the Malay singer Ramli Sarip, who has enjoyed success both as a solo artist and with the band Sweet Charity?

Sport: Li Jiawei and Patricia Chan have both won which award five times?

History: Approximately when did the first Malay peoples arrive in the Malay Peninsula?

General Knowledge: How many stations are in use on the North East Line of the MRT?

Nature: What is the world's longest snake, which can grow up to 10 m in length and is found in Singapore?

Money and Power: What is the lower level of the judicial system called, comprised of District Courts, Magistrates' Courts, the Family Court, the Syariah Court and the Small Claims Tribunal?

Language: Name Singapore's second-largest Chinese-dialect group.

Quiz 6

Arts and Literature: What does the acoustic ceiling of the concert hall at Esplanade – Theatres on the Bay allow musicians to do?

Food and Drink: From what part of China did the chicken dish *see yow kai* originate?

Geography: Which bridge is further up the Singapore River: the Elgin Bridge or the Coleman Bridge?

Pop Culture: 'Butterfly' was a big hit for which band, featuring Jay Shotam, Benny Siow, Peter Diaz and Richard Khan, in 1972?

Sport: Which high jumper and hurdler was the first athlete to represent Singapore at an Olympic Games, in London in 1948?

History: Which British lawyer and politician employed Lee Kuan Yew at his law firm in 1950?

General Knowledge: The activities of which religious group have been banned in Singapore since 1972 as they do not swear allegiance to the state, salute the flag or undergo national service?

Nature: What percentage of mammal species have become extinct in Singapore since 1819?

Money and Power: What is the name given to the economic development area comprised of Singapore, Johor Bahru and Riau?

Language: How might someone express their total indefference in Singlish?

Quiz 7

Arts and Literature: What is distinctive about actors with the Hi! Theatre group?

Food and Drink: The juice of which leaves feature in the dessert *kueh dadar*?

Geography: Which reservoir lies to the west of Seletar Airport?

Pop Culture: Jeffridin was the lead singer with which 1960s pop group, whose biggest hit was 'Peristiwa di Awang Awang' ('Mystical Event')?

Sport: Who receives almost 50% of the prize money for winning a horse race?

History: What was the popular name of a series of London negotiations with the British over Singaporean self-rule, held in the late 1950s?

General Knowledge: What was the name of the first Methodist school in Singapore which opened in 1886?

Nature: What colour is the Oriental Whip Snake?

Money and Power: Which organisation regulates the legal profession in Singapore?

Language: In Singlish what might one do twice to emphasise the affirmative?

Quiz 8

Arts and Literature: Lim Hak Tai was a prominent member of which artistic movement?

Food and Drink: What citrus fruit is often squeezed on dishes to enhance flavour?

Geography: Belilios Road, Race Course Road and Desker Road can be found in which district?

Pop Culture: Which now-defunct Scotts Road nightclub was the first to feature topless revues when it opened in 1968?

Sport: At which venue do Balestier Khalsa play their home matches in the S.League?

History: What was the name of Singapore's first prison, built in 1847 and demolished in 1968?

General Knowledge: How long does a patent normally last for in Singapore?

Nature: What does the Little Heron usually eat?

Money and Power: Apart from the Workforce Development Agency (WDA), which other statutory board falls under the remit of the Ministry of Manpower (MOM)?

Language: When somebody says, 'My England not powderful,' what are they telling you all too successfully?

Quiz 9

Arts and Literature: Low Mei Yoke and Tan Chong Poh founded which contemporary dance group in 1991?

Food and Drink: By what name is the vegetable water convolvulus, often served with *sambal blachan*, better known in local cuisine?

Geography: In which park would you find Speakers' Corner?

Pop Culture: Who was the lead singer of the band Energy during the 1990s and more recently a panellist on the first series of *Singapore Idol*?

Sport: Wee Tian Seck was captain of the national team in which sport during the 1950s?

History: Which British political party did Lee Kuan Yew canvass for during the 1950 UK general election?

General Knowledge: How many grammes does the traditional Asian measurement the kati equate to?

Nature: According to scientific classification, which 'kingdom' has 2,000 wild species living in Singapore?

Money and Power: Which property development company has interests in Singapore's Hilton and Four Seasons hotels, and operates the franchise for Häagen-Dazs ice cream in Singapore and Malaysia?

Language: Which mollusc is generally regarded as a metaphor for cluelessness in Singlish?

Celebrity Quiz

Nancy Lam

**Entrepreneur who opened her restaurant Enak Enak in 1987,
television chef, author, and food consultant to Mahiki in
Mayfair, London**

Arts and Literature: Which variety entertainment show is associated with the Chinese festival of Zhong Yuan Jie (Hungry Ghost Festival)?

Food and Drink: What anthropomorphic name is often given to the popular vegetable also known as okra, bhindi and *kacang lindeh*?

Geography: What stretch of water separates Peninsular Malaysia from Sumatra?

Pop Culture: Which cinema used to stand on the site of what is now Cathay Cineleisure on Orchard Road?

Sport: Who won seven consecutive gold medals in the discus at the

Southeast Asian Games between 1993 and 2005?

History: Which seat did Lee Kuan Yew win in the 1955 Legislative Assembly Election?

General Knowledge: What is the name of the mausoleum, or grave, of a prominent Muslim individual that can sometimes be visited for prayers?

Nature: What man-made feature divides the Bukit Timah Nature Reserve from the Central Catchment Nature Reserve?

Money and Power: In 2005 the sum of S$5,400 was the average monthly income of what social entity?

Language: If a foreigner 'catch no ball' when conversing with Singaporeans, what is he failing to do?

Celebrity Bonus Question: Nancy Lam's famous London restaurant Enak Enak is named after the Indonesian word for what expression of satisfaction, almost certainly used at the thought of Nancy's delicious food?

Quiz 11

Arts and Literature: Which traditional, sombre Malay music genre can sometimes be heard at weddings and festivals?

Food and Drink: What is the key ingredient of *foo yong hai*?

Geography: Singapore's importance as a coal depot for steamships, and consequently a trading stop, was greatly enhanced by the opening of which North African waterway in 1869?

Pop Culture: Which band, whose debut album *Night* was released in 1997, was the first local band to receive airtime on the BBC World service?

Sport: Which badminton player was a member of Malaya's Thomas Cup winning sides of 1949, 1952 and 1955 and was also the first Asian to win the All-England Championship?

History: In which year was the first Legislative Council Election held?

General Knowledge: What is the popular name for any object that falls, or is thrown, from the upper floors of a residential block, potentially endangering the lives of those below?

Nature: If an animal is endemic to Singapore, what does this mean?

Money and Power: Which bank was created by the merger of Hongkong Bank and Mercantile Bank in 1959?

Language: Name the website dedicated to the discussion of all things Singaporean, and the celebration of the use of Singlish.

Quiz 12

Arts and Literature: Which expatriate photographer was also director of Raffles Museum from 1957 to 1963?

Food and Drink: What vegetable, often used in Chinese cuisine, has large, green, slightly bitter-tasting leaves and is closely related to broccoli?

Geography: In which Malaysian state would you find Gunung Pulai Reservoir and Pontian Reservoir?

Pop Culture: Which director's first film was the 1955 Malay-language picture *Penarek Becha*, which included the song 'Inang Baru' also composed by the director?

Sport: Which swimmer has racked up a total of forty Southeast Asian Games gold medals, spanning every edition since 1993?

History: Name the Singapore Kuomintang leader who died in the custody of the Japanese military police in 1944 and has a memorial in Esplanade Park.

General Knowledge: What was Singapore's first budget airline, launched in 2004 and now merged with Jetstar Asia?

Nature: Which organisation is dedicated to the study and conservation of Singapore's natural history?

Money and Power: Name the company, founded in 1989 by Olivia Lum, that has now become a multi-million-dollar company in the field of water treatment.

Language: Which vernacular dictionary was published by Colin Goh in 2002?

Quiz 13

Arts and Literature: Which Malay songwriter penned the popular songs 'Ibu' ('Mother'), 'Bunga Tanjung' ('Cape Flower') and 'Selamat Hari Raya' ('Happy Hari Raya')?

Food and Drink: Which successful confectionary company, producing Malay cakes, tarts and other pastries, with over thirty retail outlets in Singapore, started out in the kitchen of an HDB apartment?

Geography: Bintan and Batam form part of which island group in Indonesia?

Pop Culture: Which venue, located at the corner of North Bridge Road and Stamford Road, was most famous as a 'picture palace' showing the top movies and finally closed for performances in 1998?

Sport: What sporting activity is frequently played in the environs of country clubs?

History: Who was Sultan of Johor from 1855 to 1895?

General Knowledge: Which legendary Malay character gained superhuman strength after drinking the vomit of a river sprite?

Nature: What kind of habitat can be found in Bukit Timah Nature Reserve?

Money and Power: What is the oldest foreign bank still operating in Singapore, having opened here in 1858?

Language: Under the bilingualism policy for Singapore's education system, which language must all students learn?

Quiz 14

Arts and Literature: What fruit does Esplanade – Theatres on the Bay resemble?

Food and Drink: What is traditionally used to coat Hainanese pork chops, giving them a crunchy texture?

Geography: What did Singapore have 3,225 km of in 2005?

Pop Culture: Which band released its first album, *Time of Rebirth,* in 2004 and is noted for its unusual electronic sound?

Sport: How many golf courses are there at the Tanah Merah Country Club?

History: Which World War II Malayan Communist Party secretary-general informed on his party to both the British and the Japanese, then fled with the party funds?

General Knowledge: For which nationality is the cemetery on Chuan Hoe Avenue, near Yio Chu Kang Road?

Nature: Why have Long-tailed macaques become common in Singapore?

Money and Power: What is the name given to the total value of goods and services produced within a country during a specific period?

Language: What word would be used to describe the concept of being afraid to lose in Singlish?

Quiz 15

Arts and Literature: Which institution promotes German language and culture in Singapore?

Food and Drink: What kind of noodles are typically added to *soto ayam*?

Geography: What area of water was consumed by Singapore's first land-reclamation project in the 1930s?

Pop Culture: Who directed the *Pontianak* vampire films for Cathay-Keris Films in the late 1950s?

Sport: Zainal Abidin was a celebrated exponent of which racket sport during the 1980s?

History: Name the Javanese empire to which Temasek (now Singapore) probably paid tribute in the fourteenth century.

General Knowledge: In 1878 the first example of which kind of religious building was built in Waterloo Street?

Nature: Nee Soon Swamp Forest is the last habitat for which of Singapore's arboreal mammals?

Money and Power: In 2005 Singapore signed a Comprehensive Economic Cooperation Agreement (CECA) with which Asian country?

Language: What word is written in Tamil on Singapore's banknotes?

Quiz 16

Arts and Literature: Goh Soon Tioe was a pioneering exponent in Singapore of which Western art form?

Food and Drink: What kind of meat traditionally goes with Indonesian rendang sauce?

Geography: Which stretch of water borders Sungei Buloh Wetland Reserve to the north?

Pop Culture: Which Malay singer is known for her hit songs 'Doa' ('Prayer') and 'Gadis dan Bunga' ('Girls and Flowers') and released a compilation album of her hits called *Suatu Memori* (*A Memory*)?

Sport: What has been Singapore's most productive medal-winning sport at the Commonwealth Games with twenty-two medals in total to date?

History: What was the military wing of the Malayan Communist Party known as during World War II?

General Knowledge: How many gates make up the Marina Barrage?

Nature: What is the world's second-largest orchid that can be found at the Singapore Botanic Gardens?

Money and Power: What major trading power selected Singapore as a partner for its first free-trade agreement in 2002?

Language: Which Chinese dialect was used for teaching at Tao Nan School when it opened in 1906?

Quiz 17

Arts and Literature: Which instrument does composer Zechariah Goh specialise in writing for?

Food and Drink: What is the basis of the sauce when making a fish moolie?

Geography: Which large public housing estate can be found at the Singapore end of the Causeway?

Pop Culture: Which singer, whose career started in 1952 at the age of twelve, was often referred to as Bassy Diva on account of her low singing voice?

Sport: At which edition of the Asian Games did Singapore produce its highest-ever tally of eight gold medals?

History: Name the main Malay settlement in Singapore at the time Sir Stamford Raffles arrived in 1819.

General Knowledge: Jehovah's Witnesses, the Unification Church and the Divine Light Mission have been banned from activities in Singapore under what Act?

Nature: What is a Forest Halfbeak?

Money and Power: Name the think-tank that analyses issues that affect Singapore.

Language: In which university is the Tamil Language and Culture Division based?

Quiz 18

Arts and Literature: The poet Amallathasan works in which language?

Food and Drink: Which seafood, known officially as *Lolium temulentum*, is often one of the ingredients in *char kway teow*?

Geography: Which island is largest: Singapore or Bintan?

Pop Culture: Which other female singer formed a double act with Sakura in 1967?

Sport: What is the Malay name for the spinning top?

History: Who was the first local Anglican Bishop of Singapore from 1966 to 1982?

General Knowledge: Which national club was founded in 1948 and can be found on Scotts Road?

Nature: In what year was Bukit Timah Nature Reserve designated as a nature reserve?

Money and Power: By what name is the annual wage supplement more commonly known?

Language: Which Chinese dialect hails from southern China and is often spoken by people from Hong Kong?

Quiz 19

Arts and Literature: Which playwright, author and poet, who now lives in Canada, published *If We Dream Too Long* (1972), one of the first Singaporean novels in English?

Food and Drink: In classic beef rendang, what happens to the sauce?

Geography: Which HDB new town takes its name from the Mandarin version of Lim Nee Soon, a famous pineapple and rubber plantation owner?

Pop Culture: The instrumental 'Shanty' was the signature tune of which successful 1960s pop group?

Sport: Apart from badminton and table tennis, what was the only other sport in which Singapore won medals at the 2006 Commonwealth Games in Melbourne?

History: Which airline, founded in 1947, ultimately gave rise to both Singapore Airlines and Malaysia Airlines?

General Knowledge: Which construction, completed in 2007, created Singapore's fifteenth freshwater reservoir?

Nature: What is Singapore's national flower?

Money and Power: What is the official residence of the President of Singapore?

Language: What is the literal English translation of the newspaper *Tamil Murasu*?

Quiz 20

Arts and Literature: Theatre director Goh Boon Teck founded which theatre group in 1990?

Food and Drink: What sauce should be used for braising the pork when making the dish *tau yew bak*?

Geography: Which bridge between Singapore and Malaysia was opened in 1998?

Pop Culture: Which 2001 film, directed by Djinn, harked to the popular Malay-language vampire movies of the late 1950s, starring Maria Menado?

Sport: At which Games has Singapore won a total of twenty-eight gold medals in all sports between 1951 and 2006?

History: What Islamic Malay trading state existed between 1400 and 1511 and provided a model for subsequent Malay states?

General Knowledge: In 2005 there were 150,000 foreign workers employed in what kind of job in Singapore?

Nature: What is a Harlequin Rasbora?

Money and Power: What statutory board regulates the telecommunications and information technology industries?

Language: The first Tamil inscription, written in 1828, can be found on which building?

Quiz 21

Arts and Literature: Which Singaporean Tamil author is credited with enabling the Tamil script to be displayed on the Internet?

Food and Drink: What are the key ingredients of the Peranakan vegetarian salad *nasi ulam*?

Geography: In which HDB new town would you find Yew Tee MRT station?

Pop Culture: Who was the first Indian film director to come to Singapore to make a Malay-language film in 1933?

Sport: How many times has Singapore hosted the Southeast Asian Games and its forerunner, the Southeast Asian Peninsular Games?

History: Which political organisation existed from 1945 to 1948 with the objective of uniting Malaya and Singapore as an independent state?

General Knowledge: Which weapon, partially developed by the Singapore Armed Forces, is the first in the world to be both anti-armour and able to punch holes in brick walls?

Nature: What kind of orchid is a cross between two different species of orchid?

Money and Power: Which politician was leader of the Workers' Party from 1971 to 2001 and won the Anson by-election in 1981?

Language: In which two languages did Channel 5 begin broadcasting in 1963?

Quiz 22

Arts and Literature: Who has been the music director of the Singapore Symphony Orchestra since 1997?

Food and Drink: What colour are the leaf stems on a Chinese cabbage (*pak choi*)?

Geography: What kind of buildings would you predominantly find at Kampong Ubi?

Pop Culture: What Tamil drama serial, revolving around football, was aired on Vasantham Central in 2006?

Sport: What is Singapore's premier hockey venue?

History: What civil disaster occurred in 2004, resulting in four deaths and considerable transport disruption?

General Knowledge: From which country do Nattukottai Chettiars originate?

Nature: When is the Singapore tarantula active?

Money and Power: What object symbolises the authority of Singapore's parliament and its Speaker, with parliament being unable to convene unless it is present?

Language: Why would a worker look forward to a job that is *sup sup sui*?

Quiz 23

Arts and Literature: Written by Ivan Heng and Dick Lee, what was Singapore's longest-running play, which opened in 1997?

Food and Drink: *Bakwan kepiting* involves the stuffing of which creature with a mix of crab meat, minced pork and bamboo shoots?

Geography: The Chinese Garden and Japanese Garden lie on islands located in which lake?

Pop Culture: A. Ramli, singer of hits 'Oh Fatimah' and 'Kenangan Mengusik Jiwa' ('Memories Stir My Soul'), was the leading light of which 1960s Malay pop-music style?

Sport: Up to 2006, which sport has been responsible for the greatest number of Sportsman of the Year awards for Singapore?

History: Name the short-lived British crown colony established in 1946 that included nine Malay states but not Penang, Malacca or Singapore.

General Knowledge: Which MRT station, other than Changi Airport, was added to the East West Line with the completion of the Changi Airport Extension in 2002?

Nature: What is the popular name for an Arachnis Orchid?

Money and Power: In what way are judicial commissioners different from puisne judges?

Language: Apart from Channel 8, what is Singapore's other terrestrial Chinese-language TV channel?

Quiz 24

Arts and Literature: Which award-winning Malay playwright and poet has been resident playwright for W!LD RICE theatre group since 2003?

Food and Drink: Which southern Chinese dish is sometimes called 'minced meat noodles'?

Geography: What is the English name for the rock pillar off Labrador Point, also known as Batu Berlayar and Long Ya Men, that was blown up by the British in 1848 to widen a shipping lane?

Pop Culture: Ten-year-old Johnson Yap played which superhuman character in a 1977 film of the same name?

Sport: Frederick Benjamin de Souza won an Asian Games gold medal in 1962 in which sporting test of accuracy?

History: Name the first Arab business family, important players in the real estate sector and with a road in eastern Singapore named after them, to settle in Singapore in 1819.

General Knowledge: What is the name of the tourist attraction housed in the bomb-proof bunkers of Fort Canning Hill?

Nature: The 170 species of Pteridophyta which grow in Singapore are better known by what name?

Money and Power: What is the name given to the highest level of the Civil Service that deals directly with the Cabinet?

Language: In how many languages must students achieve a pass to gain admission to pre-university?

Quiz 25

Arts and Literature: How many stages are there in the theatre building of Esplanade – Theatres on the Bay?

Food and Drink: Apart from mutton, what other kind of meat could be used to make soup *kambing*?

Geography: Which HDB new town has a name meaning 'prosperous harbour' in Chinese?

Pop Culture: The band October Cherries, popular in the 1970s, were originally known by what name?

Sport: In which sport do international teams compete for the Thomas Cup, a competition held in Singapore three times during the 1950s?

History: Name the passenger ferry hijacked by Japanese and Palestinian terrorists in 1974?

General Knowledge: How much can a first offender be fined for jaywalking?

Nature: What percentage of forest bird species have become extinct in Singapore since 1819?

Money and Power: What is the name given to the total value of goods and services produced by a country at home and abroad, less the value of goods and services produced by foreign companies in the home country?

Language: Why should women be on their guard if they have caught the eye of a 'buaya'?

Quiz 26

Arts and Literature: Which author wrote *Rice Without Rain* (1986), *The Clay Marble* (1992) and *The Stone Goddess* (2003)?

Food and Drink: In the dish *itek sio*, which two main ingredients is the duck braised in?

Geography: Name the road that links Clementi Road with North Buona Vista Road and runs to the south of Singapore Polytechnic?

Pop Culture: Which cinema, located in MacKenzie Road, opened with a screening of *The Jungle Book* in 1946 and closed with a screening of *Jaws 3-D* in 1983?

Sport: Up to 2006, which sport has been responsible for the greatest number of Sportswoman of the Year awards for Singapore?

History: How long did it take the Japanese army to occupy Malaya and Singapore during World War II?

General Knowledge: What is special about the windows in LRT trains?

Nature: What famous earlier collection of zoological specimens now forms part of the Raffles Museum of Biodiversity Research at the National University of Singapore?

Money and Power: Which businessman, with interests in banking and hotels, was listed as Singapore's richest man by *Forbes* magazine in 2003 but passed away a year later?

Language: What does the acronym WIPO stand for?

Quiz 27

Arts and Literature: What kind of art form is the Indian tradition of *silambu*?

Food and Drink: When is a jackfruit at its best for making *nangka lemak*?

Geography: Which expressway runs to the north of Jurong BirdPark?

Pop Culture: Which martial-arts film, starring Peter Chong, was made in 1973 but not released in Singapore until 2005 because of its controversial content?

Sport: In which year was the Singapore Airlines International Cup horse race first run?

History: What do Pattani, Singora (now known as Songkhla) and Kota Bharu have in common?

General Knowledge: Bukit Panjang, Sengkang and Punggol all enjoy what kind of public transport?

Nature: Which bird, found in the wild on Pulau Ubin, is the ancestor of all domestic chickens?

Money and Power: Since independence, Singapore has transformed from a manufacturing-based economy to what type of modern economy?

Language: The expression to 'arrow' someone, meaning to pick them out, originates from the practise of placing arrows by names to select individuals in which kind of organisation?

Quiz 28

Arts and Literature: Carnatic and Hindustani are two strands of what type of music?

Food and Drink: What kind of taste sensation would you enjoy if you ate *babi chin*?

Geography: Which island, at the eastern end of the Straits of Singapore, is disputed by Singapore and Malaysia?

Pop Culture: Teng Ying Hua formed a successful pop duo with fellow singer Rita Chao in the early 1970s singing under which name?

Sport: At Kranji Racecourse, of what is the inner-track surface made?

History: How many Allied troops surrendered to the Japanese Occupation forces on 15 February 1942?

General Knowledge: Which is the most complex interchange station on the MRT system, linking three different lines once the Circle Line becomes operational?

Nature: What is a Blue Bronzeback?

Money and Power: Robert Kwan developed the franchise of which fast-food chain in Singapore, opening the first outlet in 1979?

Language: When experiencing a bowel movement, how would one describe it in Singlish?

Quiz 29

Arts and Literature: In what type of music would you hear the sitar and tabla?

Food and Drink: Pineapple tarts originated as a dish from which European colonial power?

Geography: Which large shopping mall is located at Harbourfront and faces Sentosa?

Pop Culture: What unusual singing style did 1970s pop star Sakura often demonstrate?

Sport: What is the most valuable horse race to be run in Singapore?

History: Who became Singapore's first Chief Minister in 1955 and was only in office for fourteen months?

General Knowledge: Which waterway passes above Dhoby Ghaut MRT station?

Nature: What is the natural habitat of the Wagler's Pit Viper, found in central Singapore?

Money and Power: What is the term used to describe collective negotiation between representatives of workers, employers and the government to manage labour relations?

Language: What Singlish expression suggests that one has no opinion on a matter and also isn't bothered?

Quiz 30

Arts and Literature: What organisation founded the Singapore Indian Orchestra and Choir?

Food and Drink: What kind of sauce is typically associated with the spongy coconut pancakes *apom bekuah*?

Geography: Where would you find the Siloso, Palawan and Tanjong beaches?

Pop Culture: Which popular singer released the albums *Love Me* and *Dunia Oh Dunia* (*My World*) and once did a show at Caesar's Palace in Las Vegas?

Sport: How far do horses run in the Singapore Derby?

History: What internal threat to Singapore was alleged to have been discovered in 1987?

General Knowledge: Which bridge carries the Nicoll Highway over the Kallang River?

Nature: Where does the Forest Softshell Turtle spend the daytime?

Money and Power: In which industry was Singapore's last strike, taking place in 1986?

Language: Why would a man perk up and take notice if he caught sight of a 'chio bu'?

Celebrity Quiz

Lee Wei Song

Asia-renowned Chinese music producer and songwriter

Arts and Literature: In what medium does Iskandar Jalil express himself artistically?

Food and Drink: What is the name of the Indian milky rice pudding, often embellished with nuts and dried fruit?

Geography: Sun Plaza, Canberra Road and Admiralty Drive can all be found in which HDB new town?

Pop Culture: Songwriter Shangguan Liu Yun wrote *Hang Fai Fak La!* (*Walk Faster!*) (1965) in Cantonese but it was sung to the tune of which Beatles hit?

Sport: In which month is the Singapore Derby normally run each year?

History: What was the issue that prompted the student riots known as the 'May 13 incident' in 1954?

General Knowledge: Which mythical creature has moved only once, in 2002?

Nature: Apart from its diet, what else is unusual about the Crab-eating Frog?

Money and Power: Lai Siu Chiu was the first woman to hold which judicial office in Singapore?

Language: Which one of the senses would be most affected if something was 'chao'?

Celebrity Bonus Question: What was Lee Wei Song's objective when he started Lee Wei Song School of Music in 1995?

Quiz 32

Arts and Literature: What 25-tonne instrument did the German Johannes Klais Orgelbau build for the concert hall at Esplanade – Theatres on the Bay?

Food and Drink: Name the dish that, according to legend, contains eighteen different ingredients, each one representing one of Buddha's disciples.

Geography: Which bridge is further down the Singapore River: Read Bridge or Ord Bridge?

Pop Culture: Which band's best-known song is the 1991 hit 'So Happy'?

Sport: In which team sport has Singapore won twenty-one consecutive gold medals at the Southeast Asian Games since 1965?

History: Which current politician orchestrated the rescue operation for the 1983 cable car disaster?

General Knowledge: At what kind of institution do students typically study for their General Certificate of Education Advanced (GCE 'A') level examinations?

Nature: Of which class of semi-aquatic animal can twenty-nine wild species be found in Singapore?

Money and Power: What major attraction on Sentosa is owned by the Haw Par Corporation?

Language: In literal English terms, how would one rate the intelligence of an 'ah beng'?

Quiz 33

Arts and Literature: In 1991 Roger Jenkins was one of the co-founders of which comedy improvisation group?

Food and Drink: What dessert ingredient should be boiled until almost, but not quite, translucent for best effect?

Geography: Which MRT station would you use to get to Singapore Turf Club?

Pop Culture: Pierre Balmain designed the world-famous *sarong kebaya* outfit for which iconic national customer-service personnel?

Sport: In which month is the Singapore Open Golf Championship normally held each year?

History: What ended for Singapore on 16 September 1963?

General Knowledge: What new educational establishment was created from the merger of the Jurong and Outram institutes in 2004?

Nature: Where did the Changeable Lizard originally come from?

Money and Power: Gloria Lee, founder of Kim Eng Securities, was the first woman in Singapore to become a financial professional in what field?

Language: If a gentleman goes out for the evening and returns 'dulan', what has he over-indulged in?

Quiz 34

Arts and Literature: Which lawyer and famous son of a famous father published the novels *Raffles Place Ragtime* (1988) and *Abraham's Promise* (1995)?

Food and Drink: What kind of nuts are found in the dessert *foo chok pak kor*?

Geography: Which expressway divides Punggol and Sengkang HDB new towns?

Pop Culture: Which awards are handed out annually for the year's greatest achievements in the Asian film industry at the Singapore International Film Festival?

Sport: In which year was the National Tenpin Bowling League established?

History: What symbolic figure was created by sculptor Lim Nang Seng in 1972?

General Knowledge: What popular, everyday technology operates on the Global System for Mobile Communications (GSM) in Singapore?

Nature: How does the Paradise Tree Snake move between trees?

Money and Power: Name the law firm founded by Lee Kuan Yew, his wife and his brother in 1955?

Language: In Singlish, what superhuman attribute does somebody have if they watch everyone else do the work?

Quiz 35

Arts and Literature: Name Aliman Hassan's first novel, published in 2002.

Food and Drink: Which former port area on the banks of the Singapore River now hosts a long stretch of restaurants and bars?

Geography: Which HDB new town in eastern Singapore is named after the Malay word for the drum that calls Muslims to prayer?

Pop Culture: Which film studio rivalled Shaw Brothers in the 1950s and 1960s in its output of popular Malay films?

Sport: Which sporting event takes place every year at Duan Wu Jie (Fifth Moon Festival)?

History: From which modern country did the Alkaff trading family originate?

General Knowledge: Which bridge, completed in 1982, carries the East Coast Parkway (ECP) across the mouth of Marina Bay?

Nature: What is the largest mammal, other than man, that can be seen in the Bukit Timah Nature Reserve?

Money and Power: Who was the first Malay to hold cabinet-level posts in government, being minister for Health, then Labour, in the late 1950s and early 1960s?

Language: How many languages must students take at school certificate-level examinations?

Quiz 36

Arts and Literature: What kind of artistic activity is *joget moden*?

Food and Drink: How will white fungus appear after being gently simmered for five minutes?

Geography: Which road connects Woodlands Road with the Seletar Expressway (SLE) and provides access to Singapore Zoo and Night Safari?

Pop Culture: Wykidd Song is renowned for style and creativity in what field?

Sport: Where were Singapore's first tenpin-bowling lanes established?

History: Which Christian denomination, under the guidance of James Mills Thoburn, arrived in Singapore in 1885 and held their first services at Middle Road Church?

General Knowledge: In which year did the Singapore Armed Forces switch to the open mobilisation system?

Nature: In which year was the Singapore Botanic Gardens established on its present site?

Money and Power: Prime Minister Lee Hsien Loong attained a first class honours degree in which subject at Cambridge University in the UK?

Language: In Singlish, what does a 'gahmen' do?

Quiz 37

Arts and Literature: Which theatre venue is located in Raffles Hotel?

Food and Drink: For which course would you serve the sweet, clear soup *cheng thng*?

Geography: Which MRT station does the Bukit Panjang Light Railway system connect to?

Pop Culture: Which instrumental pop group was active from the 1960s to the 1980s, often as a backing group, and counted John Teo as its lead guitarist?

Sport: In which year was Jackie's Orchard Bowl, Singapore's first public tenpin-bowling venue, opened?

History: Which air tragedy occurred in Sumatra on 19 December 1997?

General Knowledge: Which hospital is the only one in Singapore to be privately funded and not for profit?

Nature: What feature of the Singapore Botanic Gardens has an archive of 650,000 plant specimens?

Money and Power: From which constituency was Lee Hsien Loong returned as an MP when he first stood for parliament in 1984?

Language: What is the likely outcome of an activity if it is described as 'GGXX'?

Quiz 38

Arts and Literature: Which theatre can be found near the Singapore Indoor Stadium?

Food and Drink: What cereal gives body to the milky dessert *bubur terigu*?

Geography: White Sands shopping mall, Elias Road and Sungei Api Api Park can be found in which HDB new town?

Pop Culture: In 2000 who became the first Singaporean to sell more than 10,000 copies of her album in the local market?

Sport: Which bowling centre hosts the Singapore International Open Bowling Championships?

History: What was the initial use of the MICA Building, on the corner of Hill Street and River Valley Road, when it opened in 1934?

General Knowledge: Of which affliction does Singapore have one of the highest rates in the world?

Nature: In what year was the National Orchid Garden opened?

Money and Power: What was Lee Hsien Loong's first full ministerial post, appointed to him in 1987?

Language: What quantity does one have if it equates to 'jilo'?

Quiz 39

Arts and Literature: Father and daughter Kam Kee Yong and Kam Ning are celebrated specialists in which musical instrument?

Food and Drink: What colour would a slice of pandan chiffon cake be?

Geography: Which two expressways converge at Changi Airport?

Pop Culture: Which local singer has released the albums *Yan Zi* (2000), *Feng Zheng (Kite)* (2001) and *Wan Mei De Yi Tuan (A Perfect Day)* (2005)?

Sport: Which Singapore golf tournament is part of the PGA European Tour and has been previously won by Vijay Singh and Colin Montgomerie?

History: The death penalty was extended to cover what offence in 1975?

General Knowledge: Who composed the national anthem 'Majulah Singapura'?

Nature: At the Singapore Botanic Gardens, which garden tells the story of plant life over the course of geological time?

Money and Power: What group representation constituency does Lee Hsien Loong represent as an MP?

Language: Which Hokkien expression meaning 'sapping strength' is used to describe a minor catastrophe?

Quiz 40

Arts and Literature: In which language does author Rama Kannabiran write?

Food and Drink: Candlenuts are used in many dishes to provide what kind of flavour sensation?

Geography: Which MRT station on the East West Line lies between Tanah Merah and Tampines and provides easy access to Eastpoint Mall?

Pop Culture: Which 1960s Malay R&B group had a hit in West Germany with 'La Obe', and thus far are the only local band to have had chart success in Europe?

Sport: Which swimmer still holds the national records for 50 metres and 100 metres freestyle, even though the times were set in 1982 and 1984 respectively?

History: Built in 1820 and located on Keng Cheow Street, what is Singapore's oldest mosque?

General Knowledge: Apart from Canning Rise, at which other location are the National Archives of Singapore held?

Nature: Which Singapore spider doesn't build a web but catches victims by ambushing them?

Money and Power: Who was Chief Executive Officer of SingTel from 1995 to 2007?

Language: If an event is described in Singlish as 'liao', does it happen in the past, present or future?

Quiz 41

Arts and Literature: Sajak is a modern style of what?

Food and Drink: What device is used to extract the juice from sugar cane?

Geography: Which river bisects the Laguna National Golf Course?

Pop Culture: Who was runner-up in the 2004 edition of *Singapore Idol*, popularly known as 'Sly'?

Sport: Up to and including 2006, which football team had won the most Singapore Cups?

History: Name the World War II operation conducted by the Japanese occupying forces, in which many Singaporeans died, to round up and eliminate suspected subversive elements.

General Knowledge: The affliction *Otitis externa*, which is common in tropical climates and causes a swelling of the auditory canal, is better known by what name?

Nature: In what behaviour does the Large-billed Crow differ from the House Crow?

Money and Power: What does the division of the Singapore Exchange known as SGX-DT trade in?

Language: In Malay, from what other language has the word *utara* (meaning 'north') been borrowed?

Quiz 42

Arts and Literature: Which composer's works have been performed by the Singapore Symphony Orchestra, Malaysian Philharmonic Orchestra and BBC Symphony Orchestra?

Food and Drink: In what form would the fruit *assam gelugor* typically be sold?

Geography: Nanyang Polytechnic is located in which HDB new town?

Pop Culture: Who was the director of the film *15* (2003) which studied the lives of young people and included scenes about youth gangs?

Sport: Which swimmer set Southeast Asian Games women's records in both freestyle and individual medley at the 1999 Games in Brunei?

History: 'S1' was the first issue, in 1906, of what everyday object?

General Knowledge: What is the highest civilian honour that can be awarded on National Day?

Nature: What does the Daddy-longlegs Spider do to put off predators?

Money and Power: Which constituency does Minister Mentor Lee Kuan Yew represent as an MP?

Language: What does the acronym OTOT stand for?

Quiz 43

Arts and Literature: What kind of musical instrument is a kompang?

Food and Drink: Beancurd or tofu is formed from what liquid once it has coagulated?

Geography: In which area would you find Lorong Chuan, Burghley Drive and Carisbrooke Grove?

Pop Culture: Which actress moved on from appearing in Lux soap commercials to starring in the films *Liang Po Po Chong Chu Jiang Hu* (*Liang Po Po The Movie*) (1999) and *Haizi Shu* (*The Tree*) (2001)?

Sport: Which Singapore weightlifter's score of 322 kilogrammes in the men's combined 56 kilogrammes class is still a Commonwealth Games record, even though it was set in 1962?

History: What product, popular all over the world, was first manufactured locally in Singapore in 1926?

General Knowledge: What part of the Singapore national flag represents the country as a young nation?

Nature: Which spider has zigzag pieces of white silk in the middle of its web?

Money and Power: How many election victories did Lee Kuan Yew win as leader of the People's Action Party (PAP) between Separation in 1965 and his resignation as prime minister in 1990?

Language: Why would someone be afraid of a 'qia zha bo'?

Quiz 44

Arts and Literature: Which playwright wrote the award-winning plays *The Bridge* (1982), *Trial* (1982) and *Emily of Emerald Hill* (1984)?

Food and Drink: What can red or white fermented beancurd be used as?

Geography: Which river separates Ang Mo Kio from Bishan?

Pop Culture: During the 1960s, what events allowed customers to see performances by popular bands on Saturday and Sunday afternoons?

Sport: At which venue are the Singapore Open and Singapore Masters track and field athletics championships held?

History: Exactly what was the 'Nanking cargo', carried by the Dutch ship *Geldermalsen* which sank off Singapore in 1752, and retrieved from the wreck in the 1980s?

General Knowledge: Which major medical charity foundation was established by Dr Khoo Oon Teik in 1969 and became embroiled in a major financial scandal in 2005?

Nature: Where do baby Wolf Spiders begin their lives?

Money and Power: Who was the UK trader who brought down the merchant bank Barings through his trading losses in 1995?

Language: What is one trying to do if one tries to 'sakar' somebody?

Quiz 45

Arts and Literature: Which Tamil author and playwright has written extensively for theatre, radio and television and uses the nom de plume Puthumaithasan?

Food and Drink: Beansprouts are a product of which species of bean?

Geography: Which road links Thomson Road and Upper Serangoon Road, and separates the HDB new towns of Bishan and Toa Payoh?

Pop Culture: What TV channel was broadcast during 2003 to provide public information on a particular health concern?

Sport: What is the name given to a record-breaking sporting performance, set by a team or individual of any nationality, on Singaporean territory?

History: Open for business between 1857 and 1932, which establishment once rivalled Raffles Hotel as Singapore's premier hotel?

General Knowledge: What was the name of the National Museum of Singapore up until 1969?

Nature: How does the Singapore Fishing Spider catch fish?

Money and Power: Which former Minister for the Environment represents the group representation constituency of Holland–Bukit Timah?

Language: From which Indian language does the expression 'Shiok!' originate?

Quiz 46

Arts and Literature: What was Singapore's first English-language theatre group, founded in 1945?

Food and Drink: Name the bakery chain, which opened its first shop at Parco Bugis Junction in 2000, where you can watch the bakers at work through glass windows.

Geography: Which unopened MRT station, on the North East Line, is closest to the former Bidadari Cemetery?

Pop Culture: Who was the 'Queen of Striptease' who performed an extremely risque and popular dance show during the 1950s and 1960s?

Sport: Who is the current Home United and Singapore goalkeeper?

History: Who was hanged in 1967 for the murder of Jenny Cheok Cheng Kid during a diving trip?

General Knowledge: China and Taiwan are the only countries that exceed Singapore in what attribute?

Nature: What kind of an animal is a Yellow-banded Caecilian?

Money and Power: In what line of business does the company Allgreen operate?

Language: Which UK organisation, based in Napier Road, runs a range of highly regarded English-language courses?

Quiz 47

Arts and Literature: Which Chinese-born playwright founded The Substation arts centre and wrote the works *The Struggle* (1969), *The Coffin is Too Big For the Hole* (1984) and *The Spirits Play* (1998)?

Food and Drink: What taste sensation would you expect if you ate a belimbing fruit?

Geography: Which hospital lies close to the entrance of MacRitchie Reservoir Park?

Pop Culture: On which channel was the 1984 drama serial *Wu Sua Nan Yang* (*The Awakening*), about the lives of nineteenth century Chinese immigrants, shown in Singapore?

Sport: Apart from the discus, in which other discipline has James Wong set a Singapore national record?

History: Which well-known politician had previously conducted negotiations with the terrorists involved in the 1974 *Laju* ferry hijacking?

General Knowledge: What does an individual become after completing two years of full-time military service?

Nature: Which spider makes a web of golden silk?

Money and Power: Who become the Workers' Party MP for Hougang in 1991, holding it ever since, and succeeded J. B. Jeyaretnam as secretary-general of the Workers' Party in 2001?

Language: If someone is 'sian', what overbearing sensation are they suffering from?

Quiz 48

Arts and Literature: What cultural activity does Lai Chun Yen play host to?

Food and Drink: What colour is the juice of *bunga telang* (butterfly peas) when you crush them in water?

Geography: Which adult educational institution lies to the east of Bedok Reservoir?

Pop Culture: What was Singapore's first 100-part drama serial?

Sport: Which organisation coordinates national activities in billiards, pool and snooker?

History: What was the national anthem before Singapore became self-governing in 1959 and adopted *Majulah Singapura* as its new anthem?

General Knowledge: What fitness assessment must National Servicemen undergo each year?

Nature: How do Silver Spiders catch their prey?

Money and Power: Which Orchard Road shopping mall, owned by the Far East Organisation, contains many electronics shops, and is a popular hangout for Singapore's Filipino community?

Language: What Hokkien mountain tortoise is used to describe someone who seems a little backward?

Quiz 49

Arts and Literature: In which art form has Han Sai Por won acclaim and a Cultural Medallion in 1995?

Food and Drink: What is the main flavour sensation of the fish curry *kuah lada*?

Geography: Little Guilin Lake can be found in which park?

Pop Culture: The actor and director P. Ramlee worked for which film studio from 1948 to 1964?

Sport: In which year did Singapore record its highest Southeast Asian Games gold medal tally of fifty, and highest overall medal tally of 164?

History: Name the discussion group, organised in the UK by students from 1947 to 1962, concerned with matters regarding the independence of Singapore and Malaya and sometimes attended by Lee Kuan Yew.

General Knowledge: Which line of the Mass Rapid Transit (MRT) system was the first to come into operation in 1987?

Nature: Which native wild orchid can grow up to 2 m in height and is found in areas of grass and scrub?

Money and Power: What type of judge presides over the High Court?

Language: In which two languages did Channel 8 begin broadcasting in 1963?

Quiz 50

Arts and Literature: Which art education institution was founded in 1984 as St Patrick's Arts Centre?

Food and Drink: What process should dried mushrooms undergo before they are used for cooking?

Geography: Circuit Road provides a circuitous route around which HDB estate?

Pop Culture: In the late 1980s and early 1990s, what long-running Malay-language historical drama serial proved popular with television audiences?

Sport: In which public recreation area would you find the National Sailing Centre?

History: When did Singapore's first presidential election take place?

General Knowledge: Which church holds its services at the Rick Auditorium in Suntec City?

Nature: What part of Russia do some of the migrant birds found at Sungei Buloh Wetland Reserve come from?

Money and Power: Who has been the Minister for National Development since 1999?

Language: In Singlish, what word is used to describe something that is the opposite of the way it should normally be?

Quiz 51

Arts and Literature: Which Singaporean ink painter is popularly known as the 'orchid artist' for his many works featuring the flower?

Food and Drink: What shape is a *won ton* dumpling skin?

Geography: Between Bedok and Tanah Merah MRT stations, the line runs parallel to which road?

Pop Culture: The Channel 5 television drama series *Growing Up* was set in which decade?

Sport: Where would you find Singapore's National Shooting Centre?

History: What was the codename given to the 1963 police raids against left-wing activists?

General Knowledge: What tragic construction accident took place on 20 April 2004?

Nature: During which months do migrant birds pass through Singapore?

Money and Power: Which car dealership has the franchise to sell Bentley, Chevrolet, Jaguar, Renault and Volvo cars in Singapore?

Language: If a district is described as *ulu*, where would it be?

Quiz 52

Arts and Literature: At what age did violinist Min Lee give her first concert?

Food and Drink: What do fennel seeds smell similar to?

Geography: In which industrial estate does the Singapore Post Centre reside?

Pop Culture: Which uniformed service did the Channel 5 television drama serial *Heartlanders* focus on?

Sport: What is the location of Singapore's only current ice rink, the Fuji Ice Palace?

History: Which World War II raid by Allied special forces sunk seven Japanese ships off the coast of Singapore?

General Knowledge: What colour are the number plates of cars licensed under the Off-peak Car Scheme?

Nature: When was the Sungei Buloh Wetland Reserve officially opened by Prime Minister Goh Chok Tong?

Money and Power: What scheme was established by the government in 1993 to help those on low incomes pay for healthcare?

Language: In Singlish, what letter of the roman alphabet always replaces 'X'?

Quiz 53

Arts and Literature: Which Singaporean author penned the 2005 bestseller *Invisible Trade: High-Class Sex for Sale in Singapore?*

Food and Drink: Which popular Chinese hawker dish literally means 'pork rib tea'?

Geography: What is the present-day name of Bukit Larangan (Forbidden Hill)?

Pop Culture: Name the amusement park opened in 1923 at Kitchener Road.

Sport: Which Singaporean swimmer set a world record of 22.69 seconds for the 50 metres freestyle in 1982?

History: Which Singapore hospital saw 200 staff and patients massacred by Japanese troops in 1942?

General Knowledge: Abdul Samad was the first Malay to practice what profession in the 1920s?

Nature: The tadpoles of which frog defy death by growing up in the deadly liquid traps of the pitcher plant?

Money and Power: Name the first bank set up in Singapore in 1840.

Language: What is the meaning of the Singlish expression 'no fish prawn oso can'?

Quiz 54

Arts and Literature: Whose performance art persona is Yellow Man, an individual wearing only underpants and covered in yellow paint, who passes comment on social politics?

Food and Drink: What is the only part of a stingray that is normally eaten?

Geography: Sir Arthur's Bridge carries which road across the Kallang River?

Pop Culture: Which singer's illustrious career began in 1977 with the album *Xin Hua Nu Fang* (*Wild With Joy*) and has continued to the present day with success in both Singapore and Taiwan?

Sport: Which Japanese football club fields a team in the S.League?

History: What was the objective of the Allied Operation 'Mailfist' in the final days of World War II?

General Knowledge: Which research and development park lies between Portsdown Road and North Buona Vista Road?

Nature: How old are most of the mangroves on Pulau Buloh?

Money and Power: What kind of member of parliament can take his or her place in the House without being elected?

Language: Why would a young lady take more than a passing interest in a 'yandao'?

Quiz 55

Arts and Literature: What was the professional name of Indonesian actress Libeth Dotulong, most famous for her film roles in the 1950s as the female vampire *pontianak*?

Food and Drink: A 'wood ear' is what type of natural edible growth?

Geography: Name the location of a row of popular bars and restaurants, featuring the renowned Cable Car bar, just off Kramat Road.

Pop Culture: What are the first and last names of the character played by Lydia Sum in the popular television sitcom *Living With Lydia*?

Sport: At which venue do the Young Lions play their home matches in the S.League?

History: What calamity were Sir Stamford and Lady Sophia Raffles rescued from when they attempted to return to Britain on the ship *Fame* in 1824?

General Knowledge: Which love festival is celebrated on the seventh day of the seventh lunar month of the Chinese calendar?

Nature: What is another name for the Green-winged Pigeon?

Money and Power: Which is the oldest local bank still operating in Singapore, having begun business through a forerunning bank in 1912?

Language: What does the acronym POSB stand for?

Quiz 56

Arts and Literature: Li Xueling, a luminary of Chinese classical music, was a gifted player of what instrument?

Food and Drink: Blue ginger and *lengkuas* are all other names for which root?

Geography: In what district would you find Parkway Parade shopping mall?

Pop Culture: Which 1960s pop group, bearing the same name as a TV action series featuring string puppets, had chart-topping hits with *Little Lady*, *My Lonely Heart* and *Hey Girl*?

Sport: Which current S.League club was originally founded in 1902 and played under the name Fathul Karib until 1975?

History: Which ethnic group, whose name means 'people of the sea', could be found living around Singapore's coasts and islands until almost the end of the twentieth century?

General Knowledge: Where can the Outward Bound Singapore centre be found?

Nature: In what way is the Vanda Miss Joaquim different to other national flowers around the world?

Money and Power: Bukit Gombak plays host to the headquarters of which ministry?

Language: If somebody says, 'Don't fly my kite,' what exactly do they mean?

Quiz 57

Arts and Literature: Which stalwart of The Stage Club theatre group was awarded a Cultural Medallion in 1983?

Food and Drink: In carrot cake, which ingredient is regarded as the 'carrot'?

Geography: Name the main town on Bintan.

Pop Culture: Which animal often joined Rose Chan on stage during her dance shows?

Sport: Which footballer captained the Singapore national team from 1993 to 1997 and spent part of his professional career with Ajax Amsterdam?

History: Which Christian denomination arrived in Singapore with British East India Company settlers in 1819?

General Knowledge: The motto 'Manners Maketh Man' appeared over the entrance to which military establishment, built by the British?

Nature: Which nature reserve is home to the largest tract of primary forest left in Singapore?

Money and Power: Which organisation promotes the interests of US businesses in Singapore?

Language: Which language has the government actively promoted through campaigns since 1979 in an attempt to replace Chinese dialects?

Celebrity Quiz

Ho Yeow Sun

International pop star, humanitarian
and fashion entrepreneur

Arts and Literature: Which author's works include *Rice Bowl* (1984), *Fistful of Colours* (1993) and *A Bit of Earth* (2001)?

Food and Drink: Before cooking, how should *fatt choi* (black moss fungus) be prepared?

Geography: Which road runs parallel to Bukit Timah Road, although the traffic flows in the opposite direction?

Pop Culture: Who won the Silver Screen Award for Best Director for *Love Story* at the 2006 Singapore International Film Festival?

Sport: What did the football club Balestier United change its name to when it first joined the S.League in 1996?

History: The former presence of what kind of land use made Orchard Road an inauspicious location for commercial activity until the 1930s?

General Knowledge: Which faith does Singapore's Parsi community, of around 200 people, follow?

Nature: Which two other flowering-plant names best describe the colours of the Vanda Miss Joaquim Orchid bloom?

Money and Power: In which country did Singapore open its first diplomatic mission after independence?

Language: What expression, involving public security officials and their outdated dress, is used to suggest that an idea or view is no longer relevant to the modern world?

Celebrity Bonus Question: With which well-known Haitian hip-hop musician, and former Fugees band member, did Sun collaborate on the single 'China Wine' in 2007?

Quiz 59

Arts and Literature: What feature of the concert hall at Esplanade – Theatres on the Bay is made of Tasmanian oak?

Food and Drink: At what annual celebration would the vegetarian dish *lohan chai* be served?

Geography: Collectively, what are the islands of Subar Laut and Subar Darat often known as?

Pop Culture: Which now-defunct cinema was the scene of a 1965 carpark bombing during the Confrontation?

Sport: Adeline Wee was a celebrated exponent of which sport during the 1980s?

History: Where did Lee Kuan Yew receive his secondary school education between 1936 and 1939?

General Knowledge: In which visitor attraction would you find the world's tallest man-made waterfall?

Nature: Of which class of cold-blooded animal can 110 naturally occurring species be found in Singapore?

Money and Power: Which businesswoman is Chief Executive Officer of Temasek Holdings and also wife of the current prime minister Lee Hsien Loong?

Language: Why would one not be very keen to have a 'kaypoh' living in one's street?

Quiz 60

Arts and Literature: Which ink painter and calligrapher is renowned for his prolific work featuring scenes of Chinatown and the Singapore River?

Food and Drink: What colour is the seed inside a longan?

Geography: Which waterway would you be crossing if you used Kandang Kerbau Bridge, Syed Alwi Bridge or Victoria Bridge?

Pop Culture: Which 1997 film, directed by Eric Khoo, was the first Singaporean film to be screened at the Cannes Film Festival?

Sport: At which venue do Geylang United play their home matches in the S.League?

History: Singapore's Penal Code, originally introduced in 1872, was based on which other British colony's penal code?

General Knowledge: Which airport, now a military air base, preceded Changi as Singapore's national commercial airport until 1981?

Nature: The Javan Pond Heron originates from which country?

Money and Power: The retail company Mohamed Mustafa & Samsuddin was started by which Indian-born businessman and his father in 1971?

Language: What is the name given to the Malaysian version of Singlish?

Quiz 61

Arts and Literature: Who has been the resident conductor of Singapore Symphony Orchestra since 2001?

Food and Drink: What do lotus seeds symbolise?

Geography: What large government building is situated opposite Novena Square, across Thomson Road?

Pop Culture: Which other comedian enjoyed a successful partnership with Ye Feng during the 1960s and 1970s?

Sport: What is the nickname of the S.League football club Geylang United?

History: Which British colony, comprised of Singapore, Malacca and Penang, was established in 1826?

General Knowledge: In which country in Southern Africa were Singapore Armed Forces first deployed as peacekeepers by the United Nations in 1989?

Nature: What colour is an egret?

Money and Power: What is the highest office in Sunni Islam in Singapore?

Language: What is the correct term for two forms of English, such as Standard Singapore(an) English and Singlish, co-existing in the same location?

Quiz 62

Arts and Literature: Which prolific Tamil author wrote *Kana Kanden Thozhi (I Had A Dream, Girlfriend)* (1978) and *Vellai Kodukal (White Lines)* (1994)?

Food and Drink: Which delicacy is created by placing it in a mixture of clay, ash, lime, salt and rice straw for a minimum of several weeks?

Geography: Turf City shopping mall occupies the site of what previous sporting activity?

Pop Culture: Which husky-voiced singer achieved fame through his 2002 debut album *Night Fall*?

Sport: What major domestic football cup competition was competed for between 1975 and 1995?

History: Name the Greek tanker which exploded in Jurong shipyard in 1978, causing the deaths of seventy-six workers.

General Knowledge: The affliction *Tinea pedis*, or Singapore foot, which is caused by fungal growth between the toes in humid conditions, is better known by what name?

Nature: What yellow bird can be commonly seen in Singapore's parks and gardens?

Money and Power: What educational establishment, training students in corporate and business skills, moved to a new city-centre campus in 2005?

Language: In Malay, from what other language has the word *waktu* (meaning 'time') been borrowed?

Quiz 63

Arts and Literature: Whose collections of Chinese poetry include *Shi Er Cheng Zhi Lu* (*A Journey to 12 Cities*) (1963), *Meng Tu* (*The Land of Dreams*) (1967) and *Wu Se De Hong* (*The Colourless Rainbow*) (1978)?

Food and Drink: What taste would a persimmon have if eaten before it is ripe?

Geography: On which road would you find the Russian, Saudi Arabian and Japanese embassies?

Pop Culture: How is the 'X' pronounced in X'Ho, the rebellious musician?

Sport: What is the nickname of the S.League football club Home United?

History: Who was the commander of the Allied forces in Singapore when they surrendered to the Japanese army in World War II?

General Knowledge: Which kind of Christian church, becoming increasingly popular in Singapore, advocates the power of 'speaking in tongues'?

Nature: What is the only common wild duck to be found in Singapore?

Money and Power: How many other candidates stood against S. R. Nathan for the presidency in 1999 and 2005?

Language: Which area of Singapore is reputedly where one is most likely to hear the Queen's English spoken?

Quiz 64

Arts and Literature: In which musical genre is pianist Jeremy Monteiro one of Singapore's foremost exponents?

Food and Drink: What popular Chinese food is traditionally made with the first green vegetables after winter?

Geography: Along which road would you find the embassies of Brunei, China and the United Kingdom?

Pop Culture: Which TV comedy character recorded the 2003 health conscious *SAR-vivor Rap*?

Sport: By what name were Home United known during the inaugural season of the S.League in 1996?

History: Which popular tourist institution first opened its doors in 1887?

General Knowledge: The fabled heroine Radin Mas is reputed to have been buried under which of Singapore's high points?

Nature: Why is the Zebra Dove declining in the wild?

Money and Power: What size of parliamentary majority is required to pass a constitutional amendment?

Language: What does the acronym SPG stand for?

Quiz 65

Arts and Literature: Liu Kang was an influential member of which artistic movement?

Food and Drink: What type of rice is the most widely used in Singapore?

Geography: What club lies at the junction of Whitley Road and Dunearn Road?

Pop Culture: Siva Choy was the lead singer of which R&B pop group who recorded the albums *Soul Sauce* and *Chinatown Rock* in the early 1970s?

Sport: With which government ministry are S.League football club Home United associated?

History: Who was Singapore's first president, from 1965 to 1970?

General Knowledge: How does the National Environment Agency (NEA) describe a Pollutant Standards Index (PSI) level over 400?

Nature: Which bird of prey, commonly seen in Singapore, is the official mascot of Jakarta?

Money and Power: Which umbrella organisation of trade unions and associations stands up for workers' interests in Singapore?

Language: In Singlish, what happens to some verbs to emphasise length of time or importance?

Quiz 66

Arts and Literature: Which artist has a gallery named in his honour at the LaSalle–SIA College of the Arts?

Food and Drink: What kind of rice is favoured in Indian cuisine?

Geography: Lorong Mambong and Lorong Liput form the heart of which popular dining and drinking district?

Pop Culture: In which 2001 Jack Neo film did Xiang Yun make her film-acting debut?

Sport: At which venue do the Korean Super Reds play their home matches in the S.League?

History: The ill-fated battleships HMS *Prince of Wales* and HMS *Repulse* were part of which British naval squadron attacked by the Japanese near Kuantan during World War II?

General Knowledge: In which year did Singapore's Post Office join the Universal Postal Union?

Nature: What is Singapore's largest bird of prey?

Money and Power: To which Indian company did NatSteel sell its steel business in 2005?

Language: What Singlish word, always used in negative circumstances, means 'to come into contact with'?

Quiz 67

Arts and Literature: Which Indian dancer was awarded the first Cultural Medallion for dance in 1979?

Food and Drink: What is the Malay name for compressed rice, often served with satay?

Geography: What does Holland Road become before it meets Clementi Road?

Pop Culture: Comedians Wang Sa and Ye Feng were collectively known by what name in their Hong Kong-made films of the 1970s?

Sport: At which venue do mainland Chinese football team Liaoning Guangyuan play their home matches in the S.League?

History: Established in 1823 on the site where Raffles Hotel now stands, what was the name of Singapore's first printing facility?

General Knowledge: Which is Singapore's most recently gazetted national monument, awarded this distinction on 5 February 2006?

Nature: What is the other predominant colour of the Black-shouldered Kite?

Money and Power: What is the name of Singapore's shipping line, of which Temasek Holdings is the major shareholder?

Language: Of what grammatical form is 'lah' an example?

Quiz 68

Arts and Literature: Which choreographer, awarded the Cultural Medallion in 1986, created the works *Fives* (1978) and *Birds of Paradise* (1979)?

Food and Drink: What should be done to crab claws before cooking them?

Geography: Which HDB new town won a United Nations World Habitat Award in 1991?

Pop Culture: Which UK pop group heavily influenced the 1960s and 1970s Malay music style known as Pop Ye Ye?

Sport: Until 2002, Singapore had only ever won nine medals at the Commonwealth Games, all except one in which sport?

History: What colonial state, excluding Singapore, was established on 1 February 1948?

General Knowledge: What disease was causing twenty fatalities every day in Singapore in 1911?

Nature: What is a Dwarf Snakehead?

Money and Power: Marina Bay and Sentosa will host the first two examples of what kind of development, inclusive of a casino, in Singapore?

Language: In which language does the radio station Oli 96.8 broadcast?

Quiz 69

Arts and Literature: Who confers the Tun Seri Lanang Award for important contributions to Malay literature?

Food and Drink: What does roasting sesame seeds do to the oil extracted from it?

Geography: Along which former coastal road would you find the Golden Mile Complex, the Concourse and the Plaza Parkroyal hotel?

Pop Culture: Which singer and actress starred in the 1962 film *Long Shan Si Zhi Lian* (*Long Shan Temple Romance*)?

Sport: At which venue do Sengkang Punggol play their home matches in the S.League?

History: What public disturbances took place in 1964, resulting in the imposition of a curfew and thirty-six deaths?

General Knowledge: Since 1965, how many presidents has Singapore had?

Nature: Which water bird is also known as the 'chicken bird'?

Money and Power: Which property developer was Singapore's richest man in 2006, according to The World's Billionaires List in *Forbes* magazine of that year?

Language: Which frequently used and characteristic Singlish word is spelled like its Malay form and used grammatically like its Hokkien form?

Quiz 70

Arts and Literature: Which organisation was set up to develop Chinese literature in Singapore?

Food and Drink: What green paste provides a hot, tangy experience in Japanese dishes?

Geography: According to the CIA World Factbook, Singapore currently enjoys 3rd place of all countries, behind Andorra and Japan and equal with San Marino, in what category?

Pop Culture: How many nightclubs can be found at St James Power Station?

Sport: Who was captain when the Singapore football team won the ASEAN Football Championships (formerly Tiger Cup) of 2004 and 2007?

History: Which famous department store moved to its current location on Orchard Road in 1958?

General Knowledge: What was St George's Church, Tanglin, used as by the Japanese from 1942 to 1945?

Nature: Apart from red, the Crimson Sunbird is predominantly what colour?

Money and Power: Which major department store lies on Orchard Road, next to the Marriott Hotel?

Language: What soup, literally translated as 'pepper water', is named after a word of Tamil origin?

Quiz 71

Arts and Literature: Where did the Malay theatre genre *sandiwara* originally come from?

Food and Drink: What kind of shrimp paste, originating from Melaka, keeps the shrimps whole?

Geography: Which large shopping mall, located on Raffles Boulevard, sits between the Marina Mandarin and Oriental hotels?

Pop Culture: What outdoor dance event is held every year on Sentosa?

Sport: At which venue do Singapore Armed Forces FC play their home matches in the S.League?

History: What was the name of Sir Stamford Raffles' second wife, to whom he was married from 1817 until his death in 1826?

General Knowledge: How many prisons and drug rehabilitation centres (DRCs) are there in Singapore?

Nature: What has caused the decline of the Black-naped Tern?

Money and Power: What service does NTUC Income offer?

Language: In Singlish, if one adds 'meh' at the end of a question, what is one expressing?

Quiz 72

Arts and Literature: Leong Yoon Pin is composer-in-residence for which orchestra?

Food and Drink: What spice is missing from this list of five-spice powder constituents: star anise, fennel, cloves and pepper?

Geography: What is the name of the jetty that sticks out into the Straits of Singapore halfway along East Coast Park?

Pop Culture: Who was the eponymous heroine, played by Marrie Lee, of the 1978 cult spy thriller *They Call Her—*?

Sport: At which venue do Albirex Niigata play their home matches in the S.League?

History: What drug was freely used, and even manufactured, in Singapore from 1819 to the late 1940s?

General Knowledge: The sale of which drug contributed to most of the colonial government's revenue throughout the nineteenth century?

Nature: Which large reptile is commonly encountered in Sungei Buloh Wetland Reserve?

Money and Power: What age must one be to become a member of parliament in Singapore?

Language: In Singlish, if somebody 'opens a light' what exactly are they doing?

Quiz 73

Arts and Literature: Which Malay poet, a founding member of ASAS 50, published the poetry anthologies *Awan Putih* (*White Cloud*) (1958), *Dalam Makna* (*Meaning*) (1984) and *Suasana Senja* (*Evening Ambience*) (2003)?

Food and Drink: What kind of sauce is frequently added to boiled eggs in Chinese cuisine?

Geography: Which hotel is two blocks away from both St Andrew's Cathedral and the Cathedral of the Good Shepherd?

Pop Culture: Which 2004 Mandarin Chinese-language television drama serial centred on the sport of swimming?

Sport: What is the mascot for the S.League football club Tampines Rovers?

History: Before being appointed lieutenant-governor of Bencoolen, Sir Stamford Raffles was also lieutenant-governor of which Indonesian island?

General Knowledge: Which is the only religious public holiday in Singapore to be celebrated on the same date every year?

Nature: Why is the Malaysian Plover unusual amongst shore birds?

Money and Power: Who is the founder and CEO of the Club 21 fashion boutiques?

Language: What does the acronym CNB stand for?

Quiz 74

Arts and Literature: Brother Joseph McNally, founder of the LaSalle–SIA College of the Arts, was a noted practitioner of which art form?

Food and Drink: What is the Chinese name for ribbon-like, flat wheat noodles?

Geography: Which hotel can be found at the corner of Prinsep Street and Bras Basah Road?

Pop Culture: Tan Ah Teck was played by which actor in the popular sitcom *Under One Roof*?

Sport: What is the name of the Under-23 Singapore national football team that competes in the S.League?

History: Sir Stamford Raffles is generally regarded as the founder of Singapore but how many times did he actually visit?

General Knowledge: The new National Library was opened on 12 November 2005, exactly the same day as the original National Library, but how many years later?

Nature: What part of the Common Redshank is red?

Money and Power: Which Singaporean company has created a successful international business, selling massage chairs and other lifestyle products?

Language: What does the acronym ORD stand for?

Celebrity Quiz

Benny Ong

'In glowing with the flow, creativity is shared'
—the philosophy of this eminent fashion designer

Arts and Literature: Which author, an intermittent visitor to Raffles Hotel, wrote the novels *Of Human Bondage* (1915) and *The Razor's Edge* (1944)?

Food and Drink: Which much-used orange ingredient is capable of permanent staining if not cleaned up straight away?

Geography: Which place of learning is located between the Singapore History Museum and the Singapore Art Museum?

Pop Culture: Which wuxia martial arts television drama serial, starring Christopher Lee and Fann Wong, was a big hit in 1998?

Sport: How many times have Tampines Rovers been S.League champions up to the end of the 2006 season?

History: In which Asian language was Sir Stamford Raffles a fluent speaker?

General Knowledge: What do the New Year's Day, Labour Day and National Day public holidays have in common?

Nature: What is a Ruddy Turnstone?

Money and Power: Which politician and gifted musician became Singapore's fifth president in 1993?

Language: What does the acronym MDA stand for?

Celebrity Bonus Question: World-renowned Singaporean fashion designer Benny Ong has counted three members of the British Royal Family—Princess Margaret, the Duchess of Kent and which other?—among his many famous clients?

Quiz 76

Arts and Literature: Which Malay theatre company established the Pesta Peti Putih (White Box Festival) in 1999?

Food and Drink: Name the sauce made from fermented shrimp, salt, sugar and thickeners that has a tar-like consistency?

Geography: Which popular dining and nightlife complex can be found diagonally opposite Raffles Hotel?

Pop Culture: Which television channel can be viewed whilst sitting on the bus?

Sport: What mascot was originally suggested by the S.League for Singapore Armed Forces FC before they adopted the rhinoceros?

History: Which important figure in Singapore's history was born at sea on 5 July 1781 in the West Indies and died in London in 1826?

General Knowledge: How many public holidays are there each year in Singapore?

Nature: How does the White-winged Tern feed?

Money and Power: What does 'OG' in OG Department Store stand for?

Language: What phrase might be added to the end of a Singlish warning about the consequences of not taking advice?

Quiz 77

Arts and Literature: What does MICA stand for?

Food and Drink: What kind of rice has soft and sticky grains after cooking?

Geography: Which shopping mall lies between OG Orchard and Orchard Emerald malls?

Pop Culture: In *Living With Lydia*, what is Lydia sometimes called due to enforced closure of her previous restaurant business in Hong Kong after a health scare?

Sport: Which football club has never finished lower than fourth place in the S.League?

History: How many of Sir Stamford and Lady Sophia Raffles' four children survived to become adults?

General Knowledge: At the Chinese festival of Qing Ming, to whom are respects paid?

Nature: What is the predominant colour of the Pink-necked Pigeon?

Money and Power: The collapse of which company caused the Stock Exchange of Singapore to be closed for the only time in its history in 1985?

Language: What does the acronym PUB stand for?

Quiz 78

Arts and Literature: Which contemporary art institution was founded in 1964 to foster 'the art of its time'?

Food and Drink: What sort of wine is Shaoxing wine?

Geography: Which shopping mall lies between Delfi Orchard and Palais Renaissance malls?

Pop Culture: In *Living With Lydia*, what is the speciality product of Billy B. Ong's seafood business?

Sport: What was the first foreign football team to compete in the S.League, lasting three seasons from 2003 to 2005?

History: Of which current educational institution did Raffles College, founded in 1928, ultimately become a part?

General Knowledge: In the story of Radin Mas, where is her father, Pangeran, left to die?

Nature: On what part of its body are the Spotted Dove's spots?

Money and Power: Once a Bill has been passed by parliament and becomes law, what is it known as?

Language: What does the acronym RJC stand for?

Quiz 79

Arts and Literature: Ang Chwee Chai was a celebrated exponent of which visual art form?

Food and Drink: What is the only way to legally import and sell chewing gum?

Geography: Which stretch of water divides Singapore from Batam and Bintan?

Pop Culture: Reggie Verghese, Hans Hussein, Benny Chan and Amir Samsoeddin were the original line-up of which 1960s pop group?

Sport: In *gasing uri*, what is the object of the game?

History: Which agreement of 1824 confirmed that Singapore would come under the colonial control of the British East India Company?

General Knowledge: St Andrew's Cathedral is associated with which Christian denomination?

Nature: How many reservoirs can be found in the Central Catchment Nature Reserve?

Money and Power: Speculation on which currency sparked the Asian financial crisis of 1997?

Language: What does the acronym COE stand for?

Quiz 80

Arts and Literature: Liu Huchen is an accomplished actor in which area of the performing arts?

Food and Drink: What type of rice is best for making congee?

Geography: Which esteemed horticultural institution stretches all the way from Napier Road to Bukit Timah Road?

Pop Culture: Who released the solo albums *Nite Songs in Day-glo* (1989) and *PunkMonkHunk* (1994)?

Sport: At which venue do Home United play their home matches in the S.League?

History: Which text, written by Portuguese scholar Tomé Pires in the sixteenth century, contains descriptions of Singapore from that era?

General Knowledge: Approximately how many kilogrammes equate to the traditional weight measure of one picul?

Nature: How does the Crested Serpent Eagle indicate its territory to other eagles?

Money and Power: To which nation was S. R. Nathan ambassador from 1990 to 1996?

Language: The grammar of Singlish is closely related to which language?

Quiz 81

Arts and Literature: Which author, a founding member of ASAS 50, wrote *Mail Mau Kawin* (*Mail Wants To Marry*) (1976) and *Syarifah* (1998)?

Food and Drink: In what traditional Indonesian salad dish are many of the vegetables pre-cooked?

Geography: Which hospital can be found on Napier Road?

Pop Culture: Adrian Pang and Fiona Xie starred in which TV sitcom about the exploits of a con artist and a ghostly bride?

Sport: Which Croatian-born striker holds the record for most goals in an S.League season with forty-two and has been the S.League's top scorer five times?

History: Which world-famous comedy star from the silent movie era stayed at Raffles Hotel in the 1920s?

General Knowledge: What hazard warning system was built on Pulau Satumu?

Nature: Which way does a Blue-crowned Hanging Parrot face when perched in a tree?

Money and Power: What is the due date by which a personal income tax return must be filed?

Language: What does the acronym SSO stand for?

Quiz 82

Arts and Literature: Which single institution houses the Lee Kong Chian Art Museum, Ng Eng Teng Gallery and South and Southeast Asian Gallery?

Food and Drink: Name the Indian snack that consists of a triangular pastry encasing a mixed vegetable filling.

Geography: Which well-known food centre sits between Robinson Road and Raffles Quay?

Pop Culture: Which 2007 Channel 5 game show has Adrian Pang as its host?

Sport: In 2007 Woodlands Wellington were the first winners of which football competition?

History: The Raffles Place branch of which well-known department store caught fire in 1972, killing nine people?

General Knowledge: Which secondary school, located in Bishan, boasts two prime ministers and three presidents amongst its alumni?

Nature: Where do Long-tailed Parakeets nest?

Money and Power: Which large, Dutch electronics company has located its Asia-Pacific headquarters in Singapore?

Language: What does the acronym TIBS stand for?

Quiz 83

Arts and Literature: The Silver Screen Awards are conferred at which annual event?

Food and Drink: Which 'hairy' fruit grows in clusters of ten to twenty and has a red skin?

Geography: What does Singapore have in common with Malaysia, China, Taiwan, Mongolia, Brunei, Philippines, central Indonesia and Western Australia?

Pop Culture: Who came in 3rd place in the 2004 edition of *Singapore Idol*?

Sport: Which country was hosting the Tiger Cup when Singapore first won it in 1998?

History: Who was governor of Singapore at the time of the Japanese Occupation during World War II?

General Knowledge: Which Hindu festival was a public holiday in Singapore until 1968?

Nature: Name Singapore's only wild cat.

Money and Power: Which company operates the 4D and Toto lotteries?

Language: What affliction is suggested by the Singlish phrase 'bak chew tak stamp'?

Quiz 84

Arts and Literature: Name the Muslim musical genre where vocal groups harmonise with percussion instruments.

Food and Drink: What kind of meat, literally translated as 'fork-roasted', is often seasoned with honey, soy sauce and five-spice powder and can be eaten with either rice or noodles?

Geography: Which hill, home to a park and a small reservoir, lies between the Central Expressway (CTE) and Eu Tong Sen Street?

Pop Culture: Felicia Chin starred as which character in the 2006 Channel 8 television drama serial *Let It Shine*?

Sport: By what score did the Singapore national football team defeat Laos to create a national record win in 2007?

History: Name the female labourers from Guangdong, China, who arrived in Singapore in the 1920s and wore distinctive blue and red hats.

General Knowledge: What military designation do Tengah, Paya Lebar, Sembawang and Changi have in common?

Nature: What nest-parasitic bird has a call that sounds like Beethoven's 5th Symphony?

Money and Power: Which company operates Singapore's port, as well as many others worldwide, and is wholly owned by Temasek Holdings?

Language: Which country has the eighth-largest number of native English speakers in the world?

Quiz 85

Arts and Literature: Which artist is a distinguished exponent of ink painting, calligraphy and seal-carving and created the blue-wash Lotus series of paintings?

Food and Drink: What is omitted from curry paste to make a green curry?

Geography: What stretch of water does the Jurong Island Highway cross?

Pop Culture: Which shopping mall, on Rochor Canal Road, offers electronics and IT goods for serious technophiles?

Sport: In the game *bola tin*, how are the tins arranged before a player tries to knock them down?

History: Which Japanese commander masterminded the Malaya Campaign and ultimate fall of Singapore in 1942?

General Knowledge: In which language was the name Temasek originally coined?

Nature: What is the most common amphibian in Singapore?

Money and Power: Who was the first woman to lead a political party in Singapore when she became chairman of the Workers' Party in 2003?

Language: What does the military acronym RSN stand for?

Quiz 86

Arts and Literature: Which important collection of literature moved to new premises on Victoria Street in 2005?

Food and Drink: Intestines, stomach and blood cubes can be found in which Singaporean dish?

Geography: What MRT station lies between Choa Chu Kang and Bukit Batok on the North South Line?

Pop Culture: Which actor first rose to fame in the 1999 television drama *Stepping Out* and more recently starred in Channel 8's 2007 drama *Mars vs Venus*?

Sport: By what score did the Singapore national football team lose to Myanmar to suffer a national record defeat in 1969?

History: Which worldwide youth movement, founded by Robert Baden-Powell, was established in Singapore in 1910?

General Knowledge: How many naval bases does the Republic of Singapore Navy operate out of?

Nature: Which nest-parasitic bird has a mournful, monotonous call that gives it its name?

Money and Power: Which former minister wrote the National Pledge, which was read at his state funeral in 2006?

Language: Which form of sign language for the deaf is predominantly used in Singapore?

Quiz 87

Arts and Literature: In 1986 what happened to the National Theatre, situated on River Valley Road?

Food and Drink: In *goreng pisang*, what is the banana coated in before it is fried?

Geography: What MRT station lies between Hougang and Serangoon on the North East Line?

Pop Culture: Who won the 2006 Star Award for Best Actress for her starring role in the drama *Family Matters*?

Sport: Who is Singapore's most-capped international footballer with 123 caps?

History: What was the Ghee Hin Khongsi (The Rise of Righteousness Association), established in 1820, the first example of in Singapore?

General Knowledge: Where is the campus of the Republic Polytechnic?

Nature: The Collared Scops Owl does what at night, every ten seconds?

Money and Power: What economic event in Singapore has been sparked by such varied causes as the international oil crisis of 1973, the Asian financial crisis in 1987 and the 9/11 terrorist attacks in 2001?

Language: What family of languages does Mandarin Chinese belong to?

Quiz 88

Arts and Literature: What distinctive feature of the old Supreme Court, Fullerton Hotel, City Hall and Tanjong Pagar Railway Station was the Italian Cavalieri Rodolfo Nollie responsible for?

Food and Drink: What is the source of *agar agar*, often used for colourful jelly-style sweet snacks?

Geography: What MRT station lies between Paya Lebar and Kallang on the East West Line?

Pop Culture: The programmes of which MediaCorp television channel are the focus of the annual Star Awards?

Sport: Who is the Singapore national football team's most prolific striker ever with fifty-five goals?

History: Name the book that provides a colourful history of the Malay royal line and is thought to have first been written in the fifteenth century.

General Knowledge: Which local organisation was responsible for setting up the first World Toilet Summit in 2001?

Nature: Where does the Large-tailed Nightjar lay its eggs?

Money and Power: Which *American Idol* judge suggested to Singaporean entrepreneur Victor Sassoon that he buy the Coffee Bean & Tea Leaf company?

Language: In mainland China, what name is given to standard Mandarin Chinese?

Quiz 89

Arts and Literature: Which theatre luminary has been artistic director of TheatreWorks since 1988 and directed *Geisha* for the 2006 Singapore Arts Festival?

Food and Drink: What sweet Malay cake consists of alternating layers made with different ingredients?

Geography: What MRT station lies between Queenstown and Tiong Bahru on the East West Line?

Pop Culture: Which actress starred in the Channel 5 television drama *After Hours* and won the 2004 Star Award for Newcomer of the Year?

Sport: Who were the 2007 Asian Cup champions on whom Singapore were the only opponents to inflict a defeat in either the qualifying rounds or the finals?

History: In the Sepoy Mutiny of 1915, what was the nationality of the prisoners of war that the mutinous Bengal 5th Light Infantry were guarding?

General Knowledge: For goods vehicles and buses, what is assessed on the basis of their laden weight and the number of axles they have?

Nature: The Collared Kingfisher can be found in what type of coastal habitat?

Money and Power: What is Singapore's policy of creating earnings by investment in other countries commonly known as?

Language: Which Chinese dialect does standard Mandarin Chinese most closely resemble?

Quiz 90

Arts and Literature: What Indian classical art form do Apsaras Arts practise?

Food and Drink: What part of China does the dish chicken rice originally come from?

Geography: From which terminal in Singapore would you catch a ferry to Bintan?

Pop Culture: Which film, theatre and television actor made his film debut in *Yellow Wedding* in 1998?

Sport: Sam Goh and Patrick Wee won a silver medal together at which world championships in Helsinki in 1986?

History: Which by-election, held in 1981, saw the victory of J. B. Jeyaretnam of the Workers' Party, the first opposition victory in thirteen years?

General Knowledge: Which country can most Singapore Arabs or 'Hadramis' trace their lineage back to?

Nature: What is a secondary forest?

Money and Power: What caused Singapore's Gross Domestic Product (GDP) to fall by 8.3% in 1997?

Language: What does the acronym CPF stand for?

Quiz 91

Arts and Literature: On what everyday object have the works of artist Ong Kim Seng featured?

Food and Drink: Which Malay dish consists of boiled yellow noodles covered in a spicy gravy with soya beans, peanuts, dried shrimps and a hard-boiled egg?

Geography: What MRT station lies between Farrer Park and Potong Pasir on the North East Line?

Pop Culture: Which well-known actor has appeared in the television comedy *Phua Chu Kang Pte Ltd*, the drama serial *Growing Up* and the film *Chicken Rice War*?

Sport: In which year did the Singapore football team first enter the World Cup qualifying round?

History: Aside from the Bengal 5th Light Infantry, which other military unit was involved in the 1915 Sepoy Mutiny?

General Knowledge: Which Buddhist temple on Race Course Road is home to Singapore's largest seated Buddha, at 15 m in height?

Nature: How does the Common Kingfisher catch fish?

Money and Power: Which government-linked company is one of Singapore's largest and specialises in engineering and construction?

Language: What are homophones?

Quiz 92

Arts and Literature: Which Tamil author wrote the plays *Suguna Sundaram* (1936) and *Gowri Shankar* (1937) and the anthology of poetry *Kavithai Malargal* (*Poems in Blossom*) (1947)?

Food and Drink: What ingredient gives the soup of *soto ayam* its yellow colour?

Geography: Which country would you be in if you were at the antipodes of Singapore?

Pop Culture: The 2000 film *Chicken Rice War* is an adaptation of which of Shakespeare's plays?

Sport: In which year did Singapore host the Asian Cup finals, also the only occasion on which they have appeared in the finals so far?

History: Which hospital was assigned to treat SARS cases during the 2003 outbreak?

General Knowledge: Which famous voluntary organisation was once located in the House of Tan Yeok Nee on Clemenceau Avenue and has now moved to Bishan?

Nature: Where do Blue-throated Bee-eaters nest?

Money and Power: Which company, owned by Temasek Holdings, is Singapore's largest power generation company?

Language: Which set of characters is used for writing Mandarin Chinese in Singapore?

Quiz 93

Arts and Literature: Pan Shou was a distinguished exponent of which art form?

Food and Drink: What filling would you most commonly expect to find in *murtabak*?

Geography: What is the first island you encounter if you go due east of Sentosa?

Pop Culture: Which well-known actress appeared in the drama serials *Measure of Man* and *Women of Times* in 2006?

Sport: The brothers Quah—Kim Song, Kim Siah and Kim Swee—all represented Singapore at which sport?

History: The first case of SARS diagnosed in Singapore came from which foreign destination?

General Knowledge: Which wholesome worldwide youth organisation has its Singapore home in the Ee Peng Liang Building in Bishan and counts the President as its most senior member?

Nature: What colour is the breast of a Blue-winged Pitta?

Money and Power: Which luxury Asian hotel chain began with its first hotel in Orange Grove Road in 1971?

Language: What encoding system is used to enable Simplified Chinese characters to be keyed into a computer?

Quiz 94

Arts and Literature: What is pantun?

Food and Drink: In which Indian dish are the meat, vegetables, spices, yoghurt and rice all fried or roasted together?

Geography: Which shopping mall is located between Zion Road and Kim Seng Road?

Pop Culture: Which 2007 Channel 8 television drama serial starred Joanne Peh and Zhang Yaodong and dealt with the subjects of dyslexia and autism?

Sport: For which Swiss football club did Singapore international footballer V. Sundramoorthy play?

History: What was the profession of Benjamin Sheares, before he became Singapore's second president?

General Knowledge: Which hospital was designated as the main treatment centre during the SARS outbreak in 2003?

Nature: How does the Pacific Swallow feed?

Money and Power: Before the development of Orchard Road in the 1970s, where was Singapore's upmarket shopping district?

Language: Which language, commonly used in Singapore, is written using a script of over 40,000 characters?

Quiz 95

Arts and Literature: Which performing arts company, founded in 1955, presents traditional Malay dance, drama and music?

Food and Drink: Which Singapore organisation, founded in 1999, promotes a diet that excludes living creatures?

Geography: Which road links Grange Road with Orchard Road and passes the Traders, Regent and Orchard Parade hotels?

Pop Culture: What 37-metre-high statue can be found on Sentosa?

Sport: Who was Home United's coach when they achieved an S.League and Singapore Cup double in 2003?

History: What legal proceedings took place between 1946 and 1948 against 919 individuals?

General Knowledge: How full must a motorist's petrol tank be before he can cross the border into Malaysia?

Nature: Which bird of prey is the world's fastest flyer?

Money and Power: From 2001 to 2002, Singapore served on which United Nations body for the first time?

Language: What is the name of the Singaporean habit of changing from Mandarin Chinese to another language or dialect in mid-sentence?

Quiz 96

Arts and Literature: Name the organisation that represents the nation's photographers.

Food and Drink: In chendol, the starch noodles would typically be presented as what colour?

Geography: In which HDB new town would you find Cashew Road, Petir Road and Saujana Road?

Pop Culture: Presenter Mark van Cuylenberg is better known to the public by what name?

Sport: Which Singapore international footballer scored two own goals for Myanmar in the 1993 Tiger Cup?

History: In 1854 which two Singapore Chinese communities fought each other in deadly riots sparked by the Short Daggers Rebellion in mainland China, causing the death of over 600 people?

General Knowledge: In which year was Singapore's last household bucket lavatory finally replaced with a modern plumbed-in toilet?

Nature: Apart from flying, in what other way do Pacific Swallows defy gravity?

Money and Power: Which current Singaporean airline was born out of the Tradewinds package-tour company?

Language: What family of languages does Malay belong to?

Quiz 97

Arts and Literature: Which composer's arrangement of the National Anthem was adopted as the official version in 2001?

Food and Drink: What sweet dessert, delicious either hot or cold, consists of yam and sweet potato cubes in coconut milk and sago?

Geography: In which district would you find Netheravon Road, Cranwell Road and Wittering Road?

Pop Culture: Jamie Yeo and Andy Penders host which show on ESPN's sports channel?

Sport: Itimi Dickson and Agu Casmir have played international football for Singapore but originate from which African nation?

History: Which security organisation was established in 1819 with eleven staff and is sometimes known as *mata mata* (Malay for 'eyes')?

General Knowledge: In which language are the proceedings conducted at the Shree Lakshminarayan Temple?

Nature: Where does the Greater Green Leafbird spend most of its time?

Money and Power: Sim Wong Hoo founded which well-known electronics company in 1981 with only S$10,000?

Language: Which language, commonly used in Singapore, often affixes one word to another to change its meaning?

Quiz 98

Arts and Literature: Daguerrotypes, by Frenchman Jules Itier, of Singapore in the 1840s are the earliest local example of what visual art?

Food and Drink: What dessert dish consists of glutinous rice balls served in a flavoured soup?

Geography: Sungei Api Api and Sungei Tampines flow into the sea through which park?

Pop Culture: Who hosts Class 95FM's drivetime radio show called *Cartunes*?

Sport: Who holds the record of scoring seven goals in one football match at international level for Singapore?

History: What mode of transport did the Singapore Traction Company mainly operate in the 1920s?

General Knowledge: From which Indian state do Sikhs originate?

Nature: What is a Yellow-vented Bulbul?

Money and Power: Which Singapore company owns 49% stakes in both Tiger Airways and Virgin Atlantic Airways?

Language: In Malay, from what other language has the word *gereja* (meaning 'church') been borrowed?

Quiz 99

Arts and Literature: Which Nobel Prize-winning author, whose works include *The Jungle Book* (1894) and *Kim* (1901), said of Raffles Hotel 'the food is as excellent as the rooms are bad'?

Food and Drink: Where would you find the vegetable *bangkwang* in its natural state?

Geography: The districts of Compassvale, Anchorvale and Rivervale can be found in which HDB new town?

Pop Culture: Which guitarist has been a member of such experimental bands as The Oddfellows, Stigmata and Path Integral, not to mention creating an extensive repertoire of his own music?

Sport: Which swimmer set national women's records in both the backstoke and the butterfly at the 2006 Asian Games in Doha and 2005 Southeast Asian Games in Manila?

History: What mode of transport made its debut in Singapore in 1896 and was often referred to as the 'coffee machine' or 'devil wind carriage'?

General Knowledge: What is the highest honour that can be awarded on National Day?

Nature: Which spider builds a 3-dimensional web?

Money and Power: From which UK university did Lee Kuan Yew graduate in 1949 with a first class honours degree in law?

Language: What bodily function is described in Singlish as 'to merlion'?

Celebrity Quiz

Simone Heng

Columnist, radio DJ and TV presenter whose work is recognised regionally, from China to Australia

Arts and Literature: Which arts institution was founded by Kuo Pao Kun and Goh Lay Kuan and specialises in nurturing multilingual and multicultural expression of the performing arts?

Food and Drink: What is the source of molasses?

Geography: Bedok Park Connector connects Bedok Park with which other park?

Pop Culture: Who was the runner-up in Miss Singapore Universe 2006 who went on to co-host reality show *The Dance Floor*?

Sport: By what score did Home United beat Geylang United in the 2001 Singapore Cup Final?

History: What was the name given to nineteenth century Chinese immigrants who planned to return home once they had earned enough money?

General Knowledge: Whose works will be on view at the Singapore City Gallery?

Nature: The Greater Racket-tailed Drongo has two elongated what?

Money and Power: Who is the secretary-general of the Singapore Democratic Party?

Language: Which is the only official language of Singapore that doesn't use measure words?

Celebrity Bonus Question: Who is the only media personality in Singapore who currently works simultaneously in all three mediums: publishing, television and radio?

Quiz 101

Arts and Literature: In which field was George D. Coleman so influential on the appearance of Singapore?

Food and Drink: Which restaurant in Singapore claims credit for inventing the dish black pepper crab?

Geography: Name the Bintan ferry terminal that serves Bintan Resort?

Pop Culture: Which television actor has hosted the variety programme *Econ Nite* and also starred in drama serials such as *Fayi X Dang'an* (*Beyond the Axis of Truth*) as a retired pathologist with dementia?

Sport: Which swimmer won three gold medals at the 2005 ASEAN Para Games in Manila?

History: Which small ethnic community first arrived in Singapore in the 1820s from Persia and gives its name to a well-known church at the foot of Fort Canning Hill?

General Knowledge: What road-pricing system was set up in 1975 and was superceded by Electronic Road Pricing (ERP) in 1998?

Nature: In 1990, three individuals of which species swam across the Straits of Johor to live on Pulau Ubin until they were relocated back to Malaysia?

Money and Power: Which organisation represents the interests of banking institutions operating in Singapore?

Language: What is the traditional language of the Peranakan community?

Quiz 102

Arts and Literature: Lin Chen was an important and influential director in which area of the performing arts?

Food and Drink: What substance, produced by palm trees, is used to make palm sugar?

Geography: The Shangri-La and Orchard hotels can be found on which road, running between Stevens Road and Orchard Road?

Pop Culture: The music of which country influenced the repertoire of the percussion group Wicked Aura Batucada?

Sport: Which S.League football club began life as the International Contract Specialists in 1974?

History: Which political party was founded at the Victoria Memorial Hall in 1954?

General Knowledge: What type of weapon is a Pegasus?

Nature: Apart from its size, how can a Little Egret be recognised?

Money and Power: Who was the third president of Singapore from 1981 to 1985?

Language: Before Singlish, what was the standard vernacular of day-to-day life in the Singapore Armed Forces?

Quiz 103

Arts and Literature: Which artist is known as the Baron of Batik and in 2003 created the world's longest batik painting, at almost 104 metres in length?

Food and Drink: Name the clarified butter much used in Indian cuisine.

Geography: Which IT mall can be found on the corner of Rochor Canal Road and Bencoolen Street?

Pop Culture: Who won the 2006 edition of *Singapore Idol* and followed up by releasing a debut album titled after himself?

Sport: Which Malaysian state was Singapore's biggest rival when it contested football's Malaysia Cup?

History: At which airport did the tragic crash of Singapore Airlines flight SQ006 take place in 2000?

General Knowledge: At which hospital would you find the National Cancer Centre?

Nature: What does the Striped Tit-babbler feed on?

Money and Power: In which year did the Singapore International Monetary Exchange (SIMEX) merge with the Stock Exchange of Singapore (SES) to form the Singapore Exchange (SGX)?

Language: Which dictionary, published by the Dewan Bahasa dan Pustaka, is often regarded as the foremost Malay dictionary?

Quiz 104

Arts and Literature: Which 3-D art space can be found at 155 Middle Road?

Food and Drink: What is the Chinese term for rice porridge where the rice is boiled in many times its weight of water?

Geography: On which road, linking Orchard Road and Bukit Timah Road, would you find the Sheraton Towers Hotel, Far East Plaza and the Royal Plaza Hotel?

Pop Culture: Willie Tann now lives in the UK but is Singapore's foremost exponent of which card game?

Sport: What is the nickname of the Singapore national football team?

History: What happened to Singapore Airlines flight SQ117 from Kuala Lumpur to Singapore in 1991?

General Knowledge: What Germanic name did the Goodwood Park Hotel go by when it was first built in 1900?

Nature: What two colours predominate in the plumage of the Magpie Robin?

Money and Power: Which local company took over BP's petrol stations in 2004?

Language: Which language, commonly used in Singapore, contains approximately 50,000 words?

Quiz 105

Arts and Literature: The Society of Chinese Artists was influential in what art form?

Food and Drink: Which cuisine fuses Chinese, Malay and Indian traditions?

Geography: What is the nickname of the frequently flooded Kampong Lorong Buangkok?

Pop Culture: The 1947 film *Singapore* was a Hollywood production starring Fred McMurray and which celebrated US actress screen goddess?

Sport: Sheik Alauddin won one World Championship, three Southeast Asian Games gold medals and thirteen Singapore national titles in which martial art?

History: What is the popular yet perjorative term used for indentured labourers during the nineteenth century?

General Knowledge: In 2004 which Jurong-based church became the first in the world to achieve an ISO 9001 certificate for the quality of its management?

Nature: How do Weaver Ants attach together the leaves that form their nests?

Money and Power: Which independent organisation represents the interests of Singapore's consumers by acting as a pressure group in the area of trading practices?

Language: Kristang, the language once used extensively by the Eurasian community, was a hybrid of Malay and which European language?

Quiz 106

Arts and Literature: Seow Yit Kin is a highly regarded practitioner of which instrument?

Food and Drink: From what organ is Chinese sausage usually made?

Geography: What is the nearest shopping mall to Dhoby Ghaut MRT station?

Pop Culture: Mark Lee plays which character in Channel 5's comedy series *Police and Thief*?

Sport: In which S.League season were penalty shootouts introduced to decide drawn matches?

History: What was the name of the Sumatran Buddhist empire that controlled the Strait of Malacca from the seventh to eleventh centuries?

General Knowledge: What large object was found at the mouth of the Singapore River in 1819, and was inscribed with an unknown language?

Nature: What is the White-rumped Shama particularly good at?

Money and Power: Which office holder regulates parliamentary debates?

Language: Apart from India, in which other South Asian country is Tamil widely spoken?

Quiz 107

Arts and Literature: Which award-winning playwright's works include *Rigor Mortis* (1988), *Still Standing* (1993) and *Separation 40* (2005)?

Food and Drink: Which fruit, reputedly the most widely eaten fresh fruit in the world, has orange flesh when ripe and contains 15% sugar?

Geography: Which road links Jurong West Avenue 2 with Jalan Ahmad Ibrahim and passes by Jurong Stadium?

Pop Culture: What kind of music does the St James Power Station nightclub Dragonfly specialise in?

Sport: What is the mascot of S.League football club Sengkang Punggol?

History: Which island, located off the coast of Borneo, was part of the Straits Settlements from 1906 to 1946?

General Knowledge: Which is the oldest existing bridge across the Singapore River, constructed in 1869?

Nature: What does the Ashy Tailorbird do to hide its nest?

Money and Power: Which statutory board monitors standards in business, encourages competitiveness and regulates weights and measures?

Language: Name the script used for writing in Tamil.

Quiz 108

Arts and Literature: Which author wrote the *Eurasian Quartet—The Shrimp People* (1991), *People of the Pear Tree* (1993), *Island in the Centre* (1995) and *A River of Roses* (1998)?

Food and Drink: What family of plants are generally used in the making of grass jelly?

Geography: Into which other river does the Whampoa River flow?

Pop Culture: The retro band Jive Talkin' play most nights at which Clarke Quay bar?

Sport: At which venue do Gombak United play their home matches in the S.League?

History: From which Indian city were the Straits Settlements ruled between 1830 and 1867?

General Knowledge: At which public institution does Ah Meng live?

Nature: In what habitat does the Asian Paradise-flycatcher breed?

Money and Power: What is the name of Singapore's second-largest telecommunications company after SingTel?

Language: Which commonly used language in Singapore uses a set of 247 characters in its written form?

Quiz 109

Arts and Literature: Which newspaper established the Kelab Coretan Remaja (Youth Writing Club) for young Malay writers?

Food and Drink: What type of cooking should sesame oil not be used for because it needs to be extremely hot before it breaks down?

Geography: What prosperous aquatic attraction is surrounded by Suntec City?

Pop Culture: Zouk is the French Caribbean term for what event?

Sport: What is the nickname of the S.League football club Singapore Armed Forces FC?

History: How many wives did Sir Stamford Raffles have?

General Knowledge: What kind of military weapon is a Primus?

Nature: What does the Ruddy-breasted Crake rarely do?

Money and Power: What is the Non-Constituency Member of Parliament (NCMP) scheme designed to do?

Language: In what kind of question can 'lah' not be used?

Quiz 110

Arts and Literature: Sin Yong Hua Heng Troupe is a Chinese opera company with its roots in which Chinese community?

Food and Drink: What is the full name of the food additive E621, promoted as a flavour enhancer and allegedly cited as causing potential health problems if consumed in large amounts?

Geography: The magnitude of which attribute places Singapore between Bahrain and the Federated States of Micronesia on a list of the world's countries?

Pop Culture: Who was the host of the English-language version of the game show *Wheel of Fortune*?

Sport: What is notable about the list of S.League top individual scorers from 1996 to 2006?

History: Founded in 1871, what recreational activity was the Swiss Club originally set up to pursue?

General Knowledge: What was abolished in Singapore by Sir Stamford Raffles in 1823?

Nature: In what habitat does the Long-tailed Shrike live?

Money and Power: What was Singapore's first statutory board, established in 1960?

Language: What is the definitive reference work for correct grammar in the Tamil language?

Quiz 111

Arts and Literature: First held in 1977, which annual arts event is organised by the National Arts Council and attracts large numbers of international artists and performers?

Food and Drink: Which hot beverage, made from leaves, undergoes minimal oxidation during its processing and has a light, refreshing taste?

Geography: According to the CIA World Factbook, Singapore has nine of which kind of transport facility?

Pop Culture: *Life Line* is a television drama serial about which public service?

Sport: What is the mascot of S.League football club Home United?

History: Which outspoken politician was secretary-general of the United Malays National Organisation (UMNO) from 1963 to 1965?

General Knowledge: What activity was banned in bars and karaoke lounges in June 2007?

Nature: What colour eyes does the Philippine Glossy Starling have?

Money and Power: What kind of organisation is established to put government development strategies into practise and has to be created through an Act of Parliament?

Language: Which one of the 5 Cs is a word of Tamil origin?

Quiz 112

Arts and Literature: Which poet's published collections include *Prospect of a Drowning* (1980), *Against the Next Wave* (1988) and *The Brink of an Amen* (1991)?

Food and Drink: What is the best way to cook a white pomfret?

Geography: Lorongs 1 to 44 can be found in which hotel district?

Pop Culture: In 1981 Maggie Teng sold 200,000 copies of *Qian Yin* (*Leading Along*) in which country?

Sport: On what type of surface is lawn bowls played at the Kallang Sports Complex?

History: What was the name the British plan, to defend southern Thailand against Japanese landings in World War II, which was cancelled at the last minute?

General Knowledge: Located in Keng Cheow Street, what was Singapore's first mosque?

Nature: What habitat makes up about 45% of the area of Sungei Buloh Wetland Reserve?

Money and Power: What compulsory healthcare savings scheme operates as part of the Central Provident Fund (CPF)?

Language: In Singlish, what letter of the roman alphabet always replaces 'Z'?

Celebrity Quiz

Ong Kim Seng
Acclaimed and accomplished full-time artist,

whose works are exhibited internationally

Arts and Literature: In what architectural style was Raffles Hotel built?

Food and Drink: Name the spicy seafood dish popular in Singapore since the 1950s.

Geography: The Bayanese Malay community of Singapore originates from which Indonesian island?

Pop Culture: Which comic actor starred in the English-language television series *Mr Kiasu* but most frequently appears in Chinese-language comedy shows?

Sport: What globally practised ball game was first played in Singapore at Farrer Park in 1891?

History: In which year was National Service introduced for the Singapore Armed Forces?

General Knowledge: What is the name of the two-tone landed properties, often favoured by Western expats as residences?

Nature: Which Singaporean monkey is found nowhere else in the world?

Money and Power: Which businessman made his fortune selling pharmaceutical products and became known as the Tiger Balm King?

Language: In addition to Malay, which Chinese dialect heavily contributed to the Peranakan language of Baba Malay?

Celebrity Bonus Question: Ong Kim Seng has had his work collected by Queen Elizabeth II, the Prime Minister of China and which two secretary-generals of the United Nations?

Quiz 114

Arts and Literature: Which institution hosts the world's largest collection, at over 6,500 works, of Southeast Asian contemporary art?

Food and Drink: What is the name of the fluffy, steamed buns with meat or vegetable fillings that are often served at dim sum restaurants?

Geography: The magnitude of which attribute currently places Singapore between Norway and Bosnia & Herzegovina on a list of the world's countries?

Pop Culture: What music style blends retro hits with more modern house music and has been a popular Wednesday-night theme at Zouk nightclub?

Sport: What is the mascot of S.League football club Woodlands Wellington?

History: Which hospital began its life as a pauper's hospital at Pearl's Hill and moved at least three times before settling at its current site in Moulmein Road?

General Knowledge: Which is Singapore's oldest Hindu temple, originally constructed in 1827 and located on South Bridge Road?

Nature: What does the Olive-backed Sunbird feed on?

Money and Power: What court adjudicates on matrimonial, divorce and inheritance disputes where both parties are Muslim?

Language: What speedy form of water transport is a word of Tamil origin?

Quiz 115

Arts and Literature: Sin Sai Hong Hokkien Wayang is a company specialising in what branch of the performing arts?

Food and Drink: What ingredient is milk flavoured with in order to create the drink *bandung*?

Geography: Sungei Kangkar, Sungei Tengah and Sungei Peng Siang are all arms of which reservoir in north-eastern Singapore?

Pop Culture: Which Channel 5 television series graphically recreated actual crimes from Singapore's recent past?

Sport: By what name was S.League football club Gombak United known prior to joining the S.League?

History: Which former president of China visited Singapore several times between 1900 and 1911 to raise funds for his revolution?

General Knowledge: Which Buddhist temple and monastery, a gazetted national monument, can be found in Toa Payoh?

Nature: The Tiger Shrike migrates to Singapore from what region?

Money and Power: Which international bank, with headquarters in London, has its main Singapore office in Battery Road?

Language: The aytam is a character in which language?

Quiz 116

Arts and Literature: Which event, first held in 2006, is a platform for international visual artists?

Food and Drink: What is the barbecued meat, often given as a gift at Chinese New Year, that tastes sweet and salty and is generally flat in appearance?

Geography: In what way are the islands of Ile de Gonaive, Haiti, and Minorca, Spain, very similar to the main island of Singapore?

Pop Culture: Which official-sounding nightclub franchise, located in Clarke Quay, has its 'head branch' in London?

Sport: S.League and Singapore Cup winners are eligible to enter which Asian club competition?

History: What device was first installed in Singapore's taxis in 1953?

General Knowledge: How many people are buried in the State Cemetery at Kranji?

Nature: What is the special claim of the Orange-bellied Flowerpecker?

Money and Power: Which government ministry holds all the shares of Temasek Holdings?

Language: If a lady 'show half ball', what part of her anatomy might she be revealing?

Quiz 117

Arts and Literature: Which orchestra is based at the Singapore Conference Hall in Shenton Way?

Food and Drink: Which herb adds a distinctive, refreshing flavour to dishes but is usually too hard to consume by itself and goes by the Latin name *Cymbopogon citratus*?

Geography: The magnitude of which attribute currently places the island of Singapore 22nd, between Sicily, Italy, and Shikoku, Japan, on a list of the world's islands?

Pop Culture: Ivan Heng appeared in which futuristic 1997 film, starring Bruce Willis and Milla Jovovich?

Sport: Which former national coach was appointed the first chief executive officer of the S.League in 1996?

History: In which year did television broadcasting begin in Singapore?

General Knowledge: Which two animals appear on the state crest of Singapore?

Nature: What is the favoured habitat of the Oriental White-eye?

Money and Power: Which company manages the Singapore Government's investments in a variety of global business sectors, as well as government-linked companies (GLCs)?

Language: What possible threat of retail is often used to get children to behave?

Quiz 118

Arts and Literature: Which performing arts company regularly presents *Ballet Under the Stars* in Fort Canning Park?

Food and Drink: What colour is the seed of a lychee?

Geography: Which major Singaporean island is occasionally referred to as Pulau Ujong, after the Malay word for 'island at the end'?

Pop Culture: In what medium would you be able to follow the adventures of Singaporean superhero Jenny Quantum?

Sport: For which team did Bosnian Esad Sedjic score the first ever S.League goal in 1996?

History: In which year were colour television broadcasts introduced into Singapore?

General Knowledge: What athletic contest is competed for annually at Swissôtel The Stamford?

Nature: The Smooth-coated Otter can be found in which nature reserve?

Money and Power: In the Toto lottery, what is the minimum amount of numbers a player must choose?

Language: What kind of annoying person does the acronym KLK stand for?

Quiz 119

Arts and Literature: What was Singapore's first major art school?

Food and Drink: Which country provided the first frozen meat and dairy shipment to the Cold Storage depot in 1905?

Geography: In which HDB estate was Singapore's first Light Rail Train (LRT) system built?

Pop Culture: What simple, Mandarin Chinese musical style was popular during the 1980s, performed largely by students and chimed conveniently with the government's Speak Mandarin campaign?

Sport: Naomi Tan and Joan Huang won a gold medal at the 1998 Asian Games in Thailand in which aquatic sport?

History: Which World War II Australian lieutenant-general controversially escaped from Singapore the very day it surrendered in 1942?

General Knowledge: In which year was National Service introduced to Singapore?

Nature: At what time of day is a gecko most active?

Money and Power: Which prominent politician did Lee Kuan Yew assign to the job of drafting the Separation Agreement in 1965?

Language: According to census data from 2000, 45% of the Chinese population of Singapore use which language?

Quiz 120

Arts and Literature: Which prolific Malay playwright founded the Teater Nadi with fellow playwright Sabri Buang in 1985, and won a Cultural Medallion in 1986?

Food and Drink: What is the yoghurt-based drink popular in Indian cuisine?

Geography: Mosque Street, Pagoda Street and Temple Street all allow pedestrians to walk from South Bridge Road to which other thoroughfare?

Pop Culture: What character did Jeanette Aw play in the 2003 drama serial *Holland V*?

Sport: How many times has Singapore won the ASEAN Football Championship (formerly the Tiger Cup) up to and including 2007?

History: Which department store boasted the first completely air-conditioned store anywhere in Asia in 1955?

General Knowledge: Which famous international medical relief organisation was established in Singapore in 1973?

Nature: What is a Chestnut-bellied Malkoha?

Money and Power: Candidates for a presidential election cannot be members of what type of organisation?

Language: What family of languages does English belong to?

Quiz 121

Arts and Literature: Which performing arts company is the only one in Singapore presenting Western opera productions?

Food and Drink: Name the rice and lentil pancake popular in Indian cuisine.

Geography: What stretch of water links the Strait of Malacca with the South China Sea?

Pop Culture: Maia Lee fronts which techno music band, which has had hits with *China Girl*, *The Love You Promised* and *Sunburn*?

Sport: Which foreign coach guided Home United to their first S.League championship in 1999?

History: Which metal, mined extensively in Malaya, fuelled a burgeoning smelting industry in Singapore during the early twentieth century?

General Knowledge: In Singapore, at the Hindu festival of Thaipusam, a devotee's *kavadi* is kept in place by what means?

Nature: What is a Slow Loris?

Money and Power: What does a lottery player ask for if he wants his number selections generated automatically by computer?

Language: What is the equivalent in Malay of 'ah beng'?

Quiz 122

Arts and Literature: Which art society, founded in 1956, focuses more on themes of social and political comment rather than artistic style?

Food and Drink: What is the soup eaten at Dong Zhi, the Chinese winter festival?

Geography: What is the entertainment area that lies between the Singapore River and River Valley Road?

Pop Culture: Which acclaimed singer-songwriter records in both English and Mandarin Chinese, her notable albums including the English-language *Bored* (1997) and the Mandarin Chinese *Huxi* (*Breath*) (1998)?

Sport: Canagasabai Kunalan held the Singaporean national record from 1968 to 2001 at which distance?

History: The first Singaporean branch of which international youth organisation was established at Prinsep Street Presbyterian Church in 1930?

General Knowledge: Since 1998, what protective feature has it been compulsory to include in all new residential developments?

Nature: How many species of venomous snake live in Singapore?

Money and Power: What was K. M. Byrne's profession before entering and after leaving politics?

Language: In what language was the short-lived 1960s newspaper the *Eastern Sun* published?

Quiz 123

Arts and Literature: On what medium are works produced at the Singapore Tyler Print Institute?

Food and Drink: Which egg and seafood dish originated in the Fujian province of mainland China?

Geography: Jalan Wangi, Aljunied Road and Kampong Ampat all lead off which road?

Pop Culture: What is the name of the maritime-themed show opened on Sentosa in 2007?

Sport: By what points margin did Singapore Armed Forces FC win the 2002 S.League?

History: The Verenigde Oost-Indische Compagnie (VOC), founded in 1602, conducted a trading monopoly across Asia on behalf of which country?

General Knowledge: Which is the oldest Hokkien temple in Singapore, located on Telok Ayer Street?

Nature: An improperly prepared Palm Civet, consumed in southern China, was reputedly the cause of what disease outbreak in 2003?

Money and Power: How long does a trademark registration last in Singapore?

Language: What parts of the human anatomy, normally found in pairs, are known as *neh neh pok* in Hokkien?

Quiz 124

Arts and Literature: What contemporary art group once established a studio in a disused Sembawang chicken farm?

Food and Drink: What is the raw fish dish that traditionally ushers in Chinese New Year?

Geography: Which street was notorious for its transvestites between the 1940s and the 1970s?

Pop Culture: What popular nightlife shows were often put on at amusement parks such as Great World and New World in the 1950s?

Sport: Which golf club was formed by the merger of the Royal Singapore Golf Club and the Turf Club Golf Club in 1963?

History: The Azahari revolt in 1963 was an expression of resistance at including which country as part of the Federation of Malaysia?

General Knowledge: Which building in Handy Road, built in 1939 and recently refurbished, was regarded as Singapore's first skyscraper?

Nature: What is the name of the ecologically important tidal zone on the northeast tip of Pulau Ubin?

Money and Power: Which bank acquired Keppel Tat Lee Bank in 2001?

Language: In which script is Baba Malay written?

Quiz 125

Arts and Literature: Phan Wait Hong has been a celebrated practitioner of which performing art?

Food and Drink: Which pungent fruit cannot grow in regions where the mean average daily temperature falls below 22°C?

Geography: What is the name of the main shopping mall in Woodlands new town?

Pop Culture: Glenn Ong and The Flying Dutchman host a weekday morning radio show on which station?

Sport: Who was captain when the Singapore football team won their first Tiger Cup in 1998?

History: What distinctive type of building, used for both residential and business purposes, was commonly built between the 1840s and the 1960s?

General Knowledge: What was the fertiliser 'poudrette', used briefly by farmers in the early 1900s, made from?

Nature: What does a Pacific Swallow make its nest out of?

Money and Power: Which building, on the corner of Bencoolen Street and Rochor Canal Road, is almost wholly devoted to IT and electronic retailing?

Language: In Chinese-language dictionaries, what is the most commonly used method of ordering the characters?

Quiz 126

Arts and Literature: Known as *jianggu* or *shuoshu*, what traditional Chinese literary activity lasted as long as it took for a joss stick to burn down, and would only recommence when offerings were made to the practitioner to light a new joss stick?

Food and Drink: In which month of the year is the annual Singapore Food Festival held?

Geography: How does the Central Expressway (CTE) negotiate the Singapore River?

Pop Culture: Which Sentosa beach has been used for major public events such as the ZoukOut dance night and the Beach Volleyball World Tour?

Sport: Who was the Singapore national football team's coach for both of their ASEAN Football Championship (formerly Tiger Cup) successes in 2004 and 2007?

History: In an agreement dated 1927, Johor state contracted to supply Singapore with what commodity?

General Knowledge: What type of weapon is an Ultimax 100 SAW?

Nature: Which bird is a nest parasite of the House Crow?

Money and Power: Which of Singapore's largest local banks was originally founded in 1935 to serve the banking interests of the Hokkien community?

Language: In Singlish, what educational background would a 'helicopter' have?

Quiz 127

Arts and Literature: Which arts centre plays host to the events *Moving Images* and *Sept Fest*?

Food and Drink: What is the famous bar on Emerald Hill, known only by its number, that serves a wide selection of cocktails and other drinks?

Geography: The Kallang Park Connector links Kallang Riverside Park with which other park?

Pop Culture: Name the world's first nocturnal zoo which opened in 1994?

Sport: Which former Malaysian international footballer is also a well-known football pundit on the ESPN channel?

History: What mode of man-powered transport first appeared in Singapore in 1880?

General Knowledge: How many publicly funded universities are there in Singapore?

Nature: What is a Whimbrel?

Money and Power: In 2004 Singapore was the first Asian country to enter into what kind of agreement with the USA?

Language: In Singlish, females of which nationality are known as 'anoneh'?

Celebrity Quiz

Chandran Nair
Internationally renowned poet and
UNESCO luminary, now resident in Paris

Arts and Literature: Which traditional style of Malay poetry is usually the sung narrative of a story or concept?

Food and Drink: Which sweet-tasting fruit is sometimes known as the 'queen of fruits' and can also cause sap stains?

Geography: What MRT station lies between Buona Vista and Queenstown on the East West Line?

Pop Culture: Which hub of bars, restaurants and nightclubs was once a Catholic convent?

Sport: In which team sport did Singapore win the Asian Championship in 2005 with a 53–39 victory over Malaysia?

History: What everyday item, associated with written communication, was first used in Singapore in 1854?

General Knowledge: Which public holiday commemorates Buddha's birth, enlightenment and death?

Nature: What is a Common Iora?

Money and Power: What is the Muslim act of property donation for personal or charitable reasons known as?

Language: In Singlish, what word would be used to describe something unfashionable?

Celebrity Bonus Question: Which of Chandran Nair's poems has been published by Oxford University Press in the anthology *The Calling of the Kindred*, and has also been selected as a set text by the Cambridge Examinations Syndicate?

Quiz 129

Arts and Literature: Which form of Tamil literature has traditionally had the highest status?

Food and Drink: What colour are the feathers of the black chicken, often used to make soups for Chinese medicine?

Geography: What MRT station lies between Eunos and Bedok on the East West Line?

Pop Culture: At 165 m in height, the Singapore Flyer is currently the world's largest example of what?

Sport: What was decided at the 117th session of the International Olympic Committee, held in Singapore in 2005?

History: Who was the last British colonial governor of Singapore, appointed in 1957?

General Knowledge: What is the name given to the open first-floor area underneath an HDB block?

Nature: What does the Hill Myna excel at in captivity?

Money and Power: Which company, initially founded in Taiwan, has built its success on rice cracker production?

Language: What does the military acronym NDU stand for?

Quiz 130

Arts and Literature: Which Singaporean composer has written the greatest number of symphonies?

Food and Drink: Why should bamboo shoots be boiled thoroughly before eating?

Geography: What MRT station lies between Sembawang and Woodlands on the North South Line?

Pop Culture: Which shopping mall, on Beach Road, has a distinctive Thai feel and is the embarkation point for many buses to Malaysia?

Sport: Joan Liew is Singapore's foremost female exponent in what sport?

History: According to the *Sejarah Melayu* (*Malay Annals*), what was the name of Singapore before it was claimed by Sri Tri Buana in the fourteenth century?

General Knowledge: What type of gift is given under the Islamic concept of *wakaf*?

Nature: What bird builds an elaborate nest out of strips of grass and leaves which can be entered from the bottom?

Money and Power: What was the profession of Singapore's fourth president, Wee Kim Wee?

Language: What does the military acronym SAFRA stand for?

Quiz 131

Arts and Literature: Which Singaporean author wrote *Foreign Bodies* (1997) and *Mammon Inc.* (2001)?

Food and Drink: What Central American fruit, with a black-speckled white centre and red skin with green protrusions, is now popular in Southeast Asia and is also known as the *pitaya*?

Geography: Along which coast do Sarimbun, Murai and Poyan reservoirs lie?

Pop Culture: Which Orchard Road shopping mall is the focal point for Singapore's Filipino community?

Sport: Swimmer Thum Ping Tjin was the first Singaporean to successfully do what in 2005?

History: Name the Ming Dynasty Chinese admiral who explored much of Southeast Asia in the fifteenth century.

General Knowledge: Dr Woffles Wu is a world-renowned exponent of which branch of medicine?

Nature: Why is the Rhinoceros Frog so called?

Money and Power: Which Dutch economic guru advised the Singapore Government, between the 1960s and 1980s, how to lay the foundations of its future development?

Language: What does the military acronym RSAF stand for?

Quiz 132

Arts and Literature: What institution was formed by the merger of the Singapore Cultural Federation, the Cultural Division of the Ministry of Community Development, the Festival of Arts Secretariat and the National Theatre Trust?

Food and Drink: Which Chinese community is usually credited with creating the noodle and gravy dish *lor mee*?

Geography: What is the northernmost MRT station in Singapore?

Pop Culture: Christopher Lee and Jeanette Aw starred in which highly rated romantic drama serial on Channel 8 in 2007?

Sport: Against which top Asian opponents did Singapore play their first international football match in 1953?

History: In 1603 the Portuguese ship *Santa Catarina*, carrying highly valuable cargo from China, was captured off Changi Point by the forces of which other nation?

General Knowledge: Which branch of Singapore's military would use an F15SG Strike Eagle?

Nature: What are the two predominant colours in the plumage of the Lesser Coucal?

Money and Power: Which organisation regulates and maintains the standards of the Civil Service?

Language: According to its most prestigious dictionary, which language, commonly used in Singapore, contains over 600,000 words?

Quiz 133

Arts and Literature: Which internationally famous violinist was born in Singapore and performed with the London Philharmonic Orchestra at the age of ten?

Food and Drink: Often prawn-flavoured, what is the Malay name for the deep-fried cracker?

Geography: The Tampines Park Connector links Sun Plaza Park in Tampines with which other park?

Pop Culture: What major shopping mall lies at the heart of Bishan new town?

Sport: How many squares are there in a Chinese hopscotch diagram?

History: Which newspaper was founded by Armenian businessman Catchick Moses and first published in 1845?

General Knowledge: How many publicly funded universities are there in Singapore?

Nature: What effect is seen on the scales of the Sunbeam Snake when placed in bright light?

Money and Power: Singapore was a founding member of which international trade body in 1995?

Language: What does the military acronym ATEC stand for?

Quiz 134

Arts and Literature: Which American author wrote the novel *Saint Jack* (1976) about an American pimp in Singapore?

Food and Drink: Which large fruit has orange flesh when ripe and many black seeds at its centre?

Geography: Name the large Indonesian island, beginning with 'S', to the west of Singapore.

Pop Culture: Which shopping mall, located in Little India, is the only one open 24 hours?

Sport: What is the best part of the foot to use when kicking a *capteh*?

History: Which educational establishment, founded in 1954, was the first of its kind and can now be found on Dover Road?

General Knowledge: Which new Singapore stadium has a seating capacity of 27,000?

Nature: What deer is unique to Singapore?

Money and Power: Which statutory board aims to help workers retain their employability through training and education?

Language: What does the slang military acronym WALI stand for?

Quiz 135

Arts and Literature: Which Singapore dance company is well known for its work in site-specific dance theatre?

Food and Drink: Name the Cantonese practice of drinking tea whilst eating small portions of a variety of dishes.

Geography: Allied and Japanese war memorials once stood at the top of which hill?

Pop Culture: Huang Qing Yuan, a popular singer in the 1950s, specialised in what type of song?

Sport: Established in 1904, what is Singapore's oldest existing golf course?

History: In which year was bar-top dancing first legally permitted in Singapore?

General Knowledge: Which well-known Beach Road building was built in 1973 and is associated with Singapore's Thai community?

Nature: A *cicak* is more commonly known as what?

Money and Power: Which bank acquired Overseas Union Bank (OUB) in 2001?

Language: When it was founded in 1955, what was the only Chinese-language university outside China?

Quiz 136

Arts and Literature: Which playwright, often dealing with feminist issues, wrote *Three Fat Virgins* (1992), *Viva Viagra* (1999) and *The Silence of the Kittens* (2006)?

Food and Drink: What part of the plant does the spice saffron come from?

Geography: Apart from Bahrain, which is the only other Asian country that is smaller than Singapore in area?

Pop Culture: What major shopping mall lies at the heart of Pasir Ris new town?

Sport: In which year was the first Singapore Marathon run?

History: The 4D public lottery was introduced in which year?

General Knowledge: In which year is the Singapore Sports Hub due to open?

Nature: What is a Whiskered Myotis?

Money and Power: What type of electoral system, where the candidate with the highest number of votes wins, is used for elections in Singapore?

Language: What does the military acronym BCTC stand for?

Quiz 137

Arts and Literature: Name the arts venue that now occupies Old Parliament House.

Food and Drink: What unusual use was coconut oil put to in nineteenth century Singapore?

Geography: According to legend, what substance is the cause of Bukit Merah's red appearance?

Pop Culture: Who sang Mandarin Chinese cover versions of popular Western songs with his band The Quests in the 1950s?

Sport: What game were Prime Minister Goh Chok Tong and President Bill Clinton reputed to be playing while discussing the prospect of a Free Trade Agreement between Singapore and the USA?

History: Which World War II battle for control of Singapore's highest point took place from 10th to 11th February 1942?

General Knowledge: OUB Centre, UOB Plaza One and Republic Plaza share what national title?

Nature: What does a gecko feed on?

Money and Power: Name the arboreally inspired upmarket hotel and spa chain, founded in 1994, that opened its first hotel in Phuket.

Language: In 1975 which language did Nanyang University convert to for teaching purposes?

Quiz 138

Arts and Literature: Which Mandarin-language theatre group was formerly known as the Singapore Amateur Players (SAP)?

Food and Drink: At which type of popular establishment can you get a variety of drinks, plus breakfasts such as kaya toast and soft-boiled eggs?

Geography: Why is Bukit Merah now a misnomer?

Pop Culture: Which 1950s Saturday-morning show at the Odeon on North Bridge Road helped many popular musical artistes further their careers?

Sport: Which female tenpin bowler won the World Masters in Abu Dhabi in 1991?

History: Which Allied defence force fought the Japanese at the Battle of Pasir Panjang in 1942?

General Knowledge: What is the maximum height allowed for any building in Singapore?

Money and Power: Which political party was formed after a split from the People's Action Party in 1959, and boycotted the 1965 General Election?

Language: According to census data from 2000, 24% of the Chinese population of Singapore use which language?

Quiz 139

Arts and Literature: Which organisation supports Indian performing arts in Singapore?

Food and Drink: Which pungent fruit, usually at least 25 cm in diameter, is the largest tree-borne fruit in the world?

Geography: Which Singaporean island, off the northeast coast, is alternatively known as Coney Island?

Pop Culture: Which fictional comic terrorist character, whose name literally means 'no sincerity', has appeared in television shows such as *The Unbeatables* and *Honour and Passion*, played by Ix Chen?

Sport: By what name were S.League club Tanjong Pagar United known prior to the 1998 season?

History: Which Chinese community arrived in Singapore in the early nineteenth century from Guangdong province in mainland China?

General Knowledge: How far can you travel in a taxi on the standard flag fall rate?

Nature: Which spiny species of mammal was rediscovered on Pulau Tekong in 2005?

Money and Power: How many prize numbers are drawn for the 4D lottery?

Language: In Singlish, what letter comes between V and X?

Quiz 140

Arts and Literature: To what decade can modern art in Singapore trace back its beginnings?

Food and Drink: *Sambal blachan* is a zesty condiment associated with which local cuisine?

Geography: What name was Bukit Panjang known by in the 1980s?

Pop Culture: Which international street festival is held every year during Chinese New Year?

Sport: Kandasamy Jayamani was a double gold medallist in both the 1977 and 1979 Southeast Asian Games in which sport?

History: Father Jean-Marie Beurel built which significant place of worship in 1847?

General Knowledge: Which organisation serves the interests of Singapore's motorists and currently has over 80,000 members?

Nature: What is the driest region of Singapore with an average annual rainfall of less than 1,800 mm?

Money and Power: What is the name of Singapore's biotech complex opened in 2003?

Language: The name Chulia was popularly used from the seventeenth to nineteenth centuries to describe which ethnic community?

Quiz 141

Arts and Literature: Which movement in Singaporean art was personified by the work of Chen Chong Swee, Liu Kang, Chen Wen Hsi and Cheong Soo Pieng?

Food and Drink: In 1990 the first Crystal Jade Restaurant was in which hotel?

Geography: Singapore's cable car service connects which two places?

Pop Culture: Academically gifted Grace Quek became better known by what name during her time as a US porn star?

Sport: In which sport did Jing Junhong win gold medals at every Southeast Asian Games from 1995 to 2003, plus the 2002 Commonwealth Games in Manchester?

History: Which distinctive Mock Tudor houses were often constructed in Singapore from the late nineteenth century to the 1930s?

General Knowledge: Which medicinal oil, sold in green and white packaging, first hit the market in the 1920s and is still popular today as a handy cure-all?

Nature: What is the highest recorded temperature in Singapore?

Money and Power: Which French bank uses Singapore as its regional headquarters?

Language: What does the acronym DART stand for?

Quiz 142

Arts and Literature: Which celebrated Singaporean violinist won the Young Artist Award (Music) in 1994?

Food and Drink: Which well-known dessert essentially consists of shaved ice on top of red beans, often with a sweet sauce poured over the top?

Geography: Norite is a type of igneous rock that forms which 133-metre-high hill in western Singapore?

Pop Culture: Which Japanese record company counted Chris Ho, Najip Ali and Humpback Oak amongst its local artistes during the 1990s?

Sport: Which actor won a gold medal in wushu at the 1993 Southeast Asian Games?

History: What penal facility was first opened in 1936 and became notorious during the Japanese Occupation during World War II?

General Knowledge: What is the world's largest passenger plane that made its inaugural commercial flight between Singapore and Sydney on 25 October 2007?

Nature: What is the poisonous part of an Estuarine Stonefish?

Money and Power: What is the highest office in Singapore's legal system?

Language: Which popular, Singlish-speaking, TV comic character took lessons to improve his English?

Quiz 143

Arts and Literature: In what year was the Singapore Art Society founded?

Food and Drink: Name the Gallic-sounding bakery and cafe that has many outlets across Singapore.

Geography: Which Indian Ocean island was bought by the Australian Government from the Singapore Government in 1957?

Pop Culture: What was the name of popular singer Joi Chua's 2004 double-platinum-selling album?

Sport: Koh Eng Guan carried Singapore's flag at the 1976 Olympics in Montreal and competed in which sport?

History: Which Indian nationalist visited Singapore in July 1943 to assume leadership of the Indian National Army?

General Knowledge: What is the potentially contagious H5N1 strain of influenza, which can transfer to humans through close contact with avian species, better known as?

Nature: What is the name of the season when the weather in Singapore is predominantly rainy?

Money and Power: Which British petrochemical multinational uses Singapore as its Asian headquarters?

Language: What is the literal translation of 'Majulah Singapura' in English?

Quiz 144

Arts and Literature: Which famous Singaporean author holds a PhD in linguistics?

Food and Drink: Which fruit has a brown skin that resembles snakeskin?

Geography: Which Singapore 'new town' sounds like the Hokkien for 'red hair bridge'?

Pop Culture: Who was the winner of the first *Singapore Idol* competition?

Sport: Anwarul Haque played for both Singapore and Malaysia during the 1960s and 1970s in what team sport?

History: In what year was the Sepoy Mutiny?

General Knowledge: What military purpose did the Abingdon Tunnels, built just before World War II, serve for the British Army?

Nature: Of which class of bipedal animal can 350 naturally occurring species be found in Singapore?

Money and Power: In which year was the Association of Southeast Asian Nations (ASEAN) founded?

Language: What is the meaning of the Singlish expression 'no horse run!'?

Quiz 145

Arts and Literature: Which theatre company has its own theatre in Merbau Road?

Food and Drink: Lim Choon Ngee reputedly created which nationally famous dish in 1956?

Geography: The magnitude of which attribute places Singapore between Syria and the US Virgin Islands on a list of the world's countries?

Pop Culture: What Singapore attraction is the tallest free-standing observation tower in Asia at 110 metres high?

Sport: Which Brazilian footballer was the first player to score both 100 and 200 goals in the S.League?

History: What international organisation did Singapore join shortly after independence in 1965?

General Knowledge: At the Hindu festival of Theemidhi, what high temperature ordeal do devotees undergo to fulfil their vows?

Nature: What can a Slow Loris produce to protect itself from predators?

Money and Power: What office must also be held by the chairman of a town council?

Language: In Singlish, what lack of resolve does the acronym NATO stand for?

Quiz 146

Arts and Literature: Wee Beng Chong and Ho Ho Ying were exponents of which art movement?

Food and Drink: For how long do Muslims fast before the festival of Hari Raya Puasa?

Geography: Which Marina Bay ferry terminal closed in 2006?

Pop Culture: What mobile entertainment was popular up to the 1950s and was comprised of a projector, generator and tricycle?

Sport: Which table tennis star was Singapore's sportswoman of the year, every year, from 2002 to 2005?

History: Which British military recreational club was situated opposite Raffles Hotel on Beach Road from 1951 to 1971?

General Knowledge: Which worldwide youth organisation, with over 6,700 members in Singapore, provides wholesome activities with a background of Christian values?

Nature: What is the world's longest venomous snake that can grow up to 3 m and can be found in Singapore?

Money and Power: In what denomination are marketable securities from the Singapore Government issued?

Language: What does the acronym SME stand for?

Quiz 147

Arts and Literature: Who founded the Artists' Village in 1987 and specialised in installation and performance art?

Food and Drink: What spicy Eurasian dish often uses leftovers from Christmas Eve dinners?

Geography: How many degrees north of the Equator is Singapore?

Pop Culture: Which band is headed by Sean Lam and Lim Shu Pann and has released the albums *Erratic* (1997) and *Horizons* (2006)?

Sport: Li Li won a 2002 Commonwealth Games gold medal in which racket sport?

History: In which year did the first radio station start broadcasting from Caldecott Hill?

General Knowledge: How many tooth relics did Buddha leave for future generations, one of which is housed at the Buddha Tooth Relic Temple Singapore in South Bridge Road?

Nature: Which common, nocturnal venomous snake goes by the Latin name *Naja sumatrana*?

Money and Power: Which property company was created when Pidemco Land and DBS Land merged in 2000?

Language: What does the acronym EDB stand for?

Quiz 148

Arts and Literature: Which 1980s art movement, of Chinese, Indian and Malay backgrounds, created work to show how different cultures could co-exist?

Food and Drink: What is the name of the Eurasian meat stew that contains plenty of vinegar?

Geography: Club Street is located in which district of Singapore?

Pop Culture: Which Filipina singer founded the band Street Smart in 1985, well-known for their song 'Funny', and was also vocal coach for the 2004 *Singapore Idol*?

Sport: Mah Li Lian was Asian champion every year between 1988 and 1994 in which racket sport?

History: Under which body's jurisdiction was Singapore from 5 September 1945 to 31 March 1946?

General Knowledge: According to the Singapore census of 2000, 42.5% of the population consider themselves followers of which religion?

Nature: What human activity has badly affected Singapore's coral reefs since the 1970s?

Money and Power: CapitaMall Trust was the first example of what to be listed on the Singapore Exchange?

Language: What does the acronym MAS stand for?

Quiz 149

Arts and Literature: The Singapore Art Museum was founded as the National Museum Art Gallery in which year?

Food and Drink: Which alcoholic ingredient makes Eurasian sugee cake distinctive?

Geography: What man-made feature was Collyer Quay originally, before it became a road?

Pop Culture: Which four-piece pop group enjoyed success in the 1960s and were fronted by lead singer Susan Lim, who disappeared in Malaysia in 1970?

Sport: Which football competition, originally known as the HMS Malaya Cup, did Singapore compete in from 1921 to 1994?

History: In which year were British troops finally withdrawn from Singapore?

General Knowledge: What is Bukit Brown used as?

Nature: The main spawning time for Singapore's coral reefs is during which months?

Money and Power: What is the popular term for a waterborne gambling emporium?

Language: What does the acronym GRC stand for?

Quiz 150

Arts and Literature: What collection of artworks can be found in Fort Canning Park?

Food and Drink: Which fish tends to provide its head for fish head curry?

Geography: Name the road that links Holland Road to the former Tanglin Barracks, many of whose buildings are now occupied by antique shops.

Pop Culture: Which film about a biker and his girlfriend, directed by Kelvin Tong and Jasmine Ng, won awards at the Singapore and Stockholm International Film Festivals in 2000?

Sport: In which year was football's HMS Malaya Cup renamed the Malaysia Cup?

History: Where did Singapore's largest fire disaster take place in May 1961?

General Knowledge: The corporal punishment weapon the cane is made from what material?

Nature: Which crab, found in Singapore's waters, in regarded as the most poisonous?

Money and Power: What social security system was set up in 1955?

Language: What does the acronym ERP stand for?

Celebrity Quiz

Sir Stamford Raffles
Indefatigable and visionary founder of the Lion City

Arts and Literature: Which Malay literary movement used its work to fight social injustice and counted Masuri S.N. and Keris Mas among its writers?

Food and Drink: Which fish is commonly used in fish head *bee hoon*?

Geography: Phase One of what public works, connecting Kranji and Changi, will be opened in 2008?

Pop Culture: Which singer was known as 'Singapore's Elvis Presley' during the 1950s and 1960s?

Sport: On how many occasions did Singapore win the Malaysia Cup?

History: In 1820 members of which seafaring ethnic group, led by Arong Bilawa, founded a settlement on the Kallang River?

General Knowledge: Singapore's cable car runs between Sentosa and which other location?

Nature: Which coral-eating starfish has so far yet to attack Singapore's reefs?

Money and Power: In which year did it become no longer possible to interchange currency between Malaysia and Singapore?

Language: What does the acronym SMC stand for?

Celebrity Bonus Question: The environment of Southeast Asia provided Sir Stamford Raffles with plenty of opportunity to pursue his enthusiasm for which scientific discipline?

Quiz 152

Arts and Literature: In which year was the Arts Theatre of Singapore (formerly Singapore Amateur Players) founded?

Food and Drink: What was Singapore's most important crop between the 1830s and the beginning of the twentieth century?

Geography: What is the most westerly station on the East West Line?

Pop Culture: Which record producer established the Ocean Butterflies record label and kickstarted the careers of Kit Chan and J J Lin?

Sport: What is the oldest sports club in Singapore, having been founded as the Singapore Sporting Club in 1842?

History: What financial responsibility did Governor Sir Franklin Gimson introduce for Singaporeans in 1947?

General Knowledge: Which major commercial office development was constructed, according to *feng shui* principles, to represent a ring in the palm of a hand, with four fingers and a thumb represented by five office blocks?

Nature: What regular visitor to Singapore is the world's largest bat?

Money and Power: Which party has won an overall majority at every Singaporean election from 1959 to 2006?

Language: Apart from Malaysia, Indonesia and Singapore, which other country uses a form of Malay as its official language?

Quiz 153

Arts and Literature: Bani Buang directed *Gema Seni* (*Echo of the Arts*), the Malay production in what form of theatre?

Food and Drink: Name Singapore's first food court, which opened in 1987.

Geography: Which well-known thoroughfare ran through the centre of old postal District 9?

Pop Culture: What nude cabaret show was brought to Singapore in 2005 by the Eng Wah Organisation?

Sport: Who was the first Singaporean golfer to win a European tour title, taking the Singapore Masters in 2006?

History: What transport disaster of January 1983 resulted in the deaths of seven people?

General Knowledge: According to the Singapore census of 2000, 7% of the population consider themselves followers of which religious denomination?

Nature: In which Singaporean nature reserve have wild crocodiles occasionally been found?

Money and Power: Who was the first graduate of a local law school to become Singapore's Chief Justice in 2006?

Language: What does the acronym SSE stand for?

Quiz 154

Arts and Literature: What art form is created on cloth using a combination of wax patterns and dyeing?

Food and Drink: Name the food court on the fourth floor of Wisma Atria?

Geography: Which settlement was founded on the east coast of Peninsular Malaysia during the Japanese Occupation, and was to resettle the Chinese from Singapore?

Pop Culture: Which internationally renowned UK pop group, who played the Singapore Badminton Hall in 1961, were famous for their electric guitar sound?

Sport: In which team sport did Melanie Martens have an illustrious career spanning the years 1974–99?

History: Which 1970s national campaign was intended to slow the population growth of Singapore?

General Knowledge: Whose names would one find on the Cenotaph on Queen Elizabeth Walk?

Nature: What is the main source of food for House Crows?

Money and Power: Which company runs the largest wafer manufacturing facility in Singapore?

Language: What type of English might a Singaporean speak in formal situations?

Quiz 155

Arts and Literature: Which celebrated British author's first novel is called *Time for a Tiger*, a reference to Tiger Beer and not the big cat?

Food and Drink: Which fruit is frequently called the 'king of fruits'?

Geography: Which street in Kampong Glam is famous for its textile, spice and jewellery traders?

Pop Culture: What was the amusement park Gay World known as before its name was changed?

Sport: Which bodybuilder became the first Singaporean Mr Universe in 1993?

History: Why was the currency used during the Japanese Occupation known as 'banana money'?

General Knowledge: Which traditional Chinese medicine involves sticking needles into a patient's skin to control and alleviate pain and other symptoms?

Nature: Of which class of ovum-laying animal can 165 species be seen year round in Singapore?

Money and Power: The Association of Southeast Asian Nations (ASEAN) is comprised of how many countries?

Language: In which direction should you go if somebody asks you to 'gostan' in Singlish?

Quiz 156

Arts and Literature: On what surface are the colourful Bengali rice patterns known as alpona created?

Food and Drink: In which year was Tiger Beer launched?

Geography: What was the first expressway, opened in 1981?

Pop Culture: Which 1964 television show was a platform for contemporary pop groups?

Sport: What was the seating capacity of the National Stadium?

History: In 1998 what system of traffic management was introduced for some of Singapore's busiest roads?

General Knowledge: What is the burial period allowed at Choa Chu Kang Cemetery Complex, before the deceased are exhumed to prevent overcrowding?

Nature: What do Staghorn and Bird's Nest Ferns grow on?

Money and Power: Who has been the secretary-general of the Singapore Democratic Party (SDP) since 1993?

Language: What is the the colloquial form of English used in informal situations?

Quiz 157

Arts and Literature: Which author, born at Leonie Hill Road, created the character Simon Templar (The Saint) who featured in over one hundred books, films and TV series?

Food and Drink: What kind of food is the Khong Guan company famous for making?

Geography: Which district, host to a month-long market prior to Hari Raya Puasa, is named after the Malay words for 'lemongrass factory'?

Pop Culture: Which record company counted The Watchmen, The Pagans and The Ordinary People amongst its artistes?

Sport: In 1948 Ng Liang Chiang won Singapore's first Asian Games gold medal in New Delhi in which athletic discipline?

History: Who became the secretary-general of the Malayan Communist Party (MCP) in 1947?

General Knowledge: With the opening of Terminal 3 in 2008, how many terminals does Changi Airport have?

Nature: What does a Puffer Fish do to defend itself?

Money and Power: What is the highest-ranking office in the Singapore military?

Language: What language campaign was inaugurated in 2000?

Quiz 158

Arts and Literature: Santha Bhaskar's 1996 production of *Manohra* brought together the dance traditions of which two countries?

Food and Drink: Name the popular bar and jazz venue at the southern end of Boat Quay.

Geography: Name the military structure, dating from the 1880s, at the western end of Sentosa.

Pop Culture: What was the 'colour' of the 1970s culture, symbolised by rock music and long hair, that was discouraged with a tax on live music?

Sport: The National Stadium hosted two editions of which regional sports event in 1983 and 1993?

History: What part of his body did Colonel Orfeur Cavenagh, Governor of Singapore, lose in the Indian Mutiny of 1857?

General Knowledge: What is the big religious building, or *gurdwara*, on the corner of Towner Road and Serangoon Road?

Nature: What does a Mosquito Fern grow on?

Money and Power: For which crime did Asia-Pacific Breweries Finance Manager Chia Teck Leng receive a 42-year prison sentence in 2003?

Language: Which Chinese dialect has been the most influential in the development of Singlish?

Quiz 159

Arts and Literature: What is the first volume of Lee Kuan Yew's memoirs called?

Food and Drink: What were established in the 1960s to improve the hygiene standards of street food vendors?

Geography: What is the Jurong Formation, which covers most of western Singapore?

Pop Culture: Which local band had a hit with 'Within You'll Remain' in the early 1980s?

Sport: The Southeast Asian Peninsular Games of 1973 was the first sporting event to be hosted by which venue?

History: What first took place in Singapore in 1871 and has taken place every ten years since then, except during World War II?

General Knowledge: How long is a Certificate of Entitlement (COE) on a taxi valid for?

Nature: When was the Tilapia Fish, native to Africa, introduced into Singapore's lakes and rivers?

Money and Power: Who was detained for twenty-three years under the Internal Security Act for pro-communist activity, finally being released in 1992?

Language: In what institutions did Singlish first begin to develop during the late nineteenth century?

Quiz 160

Arts and Literature: Which British journalist, who died in Singapore in 2005, wrote *The Messiah and the Mandarins* (1982) and *Any Number Can Play* (1972)?

Food and Drink: *Rochor mee* is another name for which popular fried Singapore dish?

Geography: What type of rock is Bukit Timah granite?

Pop Culture: Philip and Michael Cheah founded which music and pop culture magazine in 1985?

Sport: What was the name given to the wave of sound created by local fans to support the Singapore football team at the National Stadium?

History: Singapore was under whose rule when Changi Airport was originally built?

General Knowledge: What do successful Certificate of Entitlement (COE) bidders pay?

Nature: Which unusual-looking upright fish is protected in Singapore's coastal waters?

Money and Power: Singapore People's Party MP Chiam See Tong represents which constituency?

Language: How many official languages does Singapore have?

Quiz 161

Arts and Literature: Which Indonesian island strongly influenced the work of the Nanyang School of artists?

Food and Drink: Why is the curry filling in a curry puff of a thick consistency?

Geography: The Causeway crosses which stretch of water?

Pop Culture: *Yi Jia Zhi Zhu* (*Crime Does Not Pay*), *Huang Tang Shi Jia* (*Hypocrite*) and *Qiao De Liang An* (*Two Sides of the Bridge*) were the only films ever made by which short-lived 1970s film studio?

Sport: Which adventurer has achieved many feats of physical endurance, including successfully scaling Mount Everest in 1998 and 2006?

History: Which major trading company, named after a large Southeast Asian island, was active in many sectors from 1856 to 1967 when it was bought by Inchcape?

General Knowledge: What type of military equipment is a Bionix?

Nature: What is the lowest recorded temperature in Singapore?

Money and Power: Which car distributor takes its name from a large Southeast Asian island?

Language: What does the acronym DSO stand for?

Quiz 162

Arts and Literature: K. P. Bhaskar is a noted exponent of which art form?

Food and Drink: *Yong tau foo* is a traditional dish for which Chinese dialect group?

Geography: What kind of geographical feature was Farrer Park in its original, natural state?

Pop Culture: Name the first local band to sign up to international record company Philips in 1963.

Sport: In which year was the National Stadium opened by Lee Kuan Yew?

History: Since 1990 which document, that applicants can bid for, has been used to restrict vehicle ownership?

General Knowledge: Which body is responsible for conducting the national census every ten years?

Nature: In which nature reserve is Fern Valley?

Money and Power: Which island is the focal point of Singapore's chemical sector?

Language: What was the lingua franca of Singapore from the late nineteenth to early twentieth century?

Quiz 163

Arts and Literature: Who founded the Singapore Chamber Ensemble and was a pioneer of Western classical music in Singapore?

Food and Drink: Curry laksa was created by which Chinese community, resident in the Malay Peninsula for several centuries?

Geography: What is the height in metres of Singapore's highest point, Bukit Timah?

Pop Culture: What is the venue for Baybeats, Singapore's indie and alternative music festival?

Sport: Which badminton player reached the quarter-finals of the 2004 Olympic Games individual event in Athens before losing out to Thai opponent Boonsak Ponsana?

History: Which 1956 protest centred on Chinese High School and Chung Cheng High School and resulted in the deaths of thirteen people?

General Knowledge: Which eminent physician became known as the 'Father of Forensic Pathology' for his expertise in establishing criminal evidence and the identification of the victims of crime and disasters?

Nature: What did a Tiger Shark, caught in Singapore waters in 1967, have in its stomach?

Money and Power: Who was secretary-general of the Malayan Communist Party (MCP) from 1947 to 1981?

Language: What does the acronym HDB stand for?

Quiz 164

Arts and Literature: Chen Chong Swee, a member of the Nanyang School art movement, was a fine exponent in which medium?

Food and Drink: Which famous French restaurant can be found on the second floor of the Shaw Centre?

Geography: What is Singapore's easternmost island?

Pop Culture: What was the name of 2004 *Singapore Idol* winner Taufik Batisah's debut album, which sold 30,000 copies?

Sport: On Shaw Ming won a gold medal at the 2006 Commonwealth Games in Melbourne in which sport?

History: Chinese Emperor Han Wu Di first added what important day to the lunar calendar?

General Knowledge: Professor Louis H. Y. Chen is an eminent international academic in which discipline?

Nature: Singapore's largest goby, the Marble Goby, is also known by what name?

Money and Power: Which fuel supply company was embroiled in heavy losses and an insider-trading scandal in 2004?

Language: What does the acronym URA stand for?

Quiz 165

Arts and Literature: Name the first Chinese daily newspaper to be published in Singapore in 1881.

Food and Drink: On what snack has Polar Cafe based its success?

Geography: Which district in eastern Singapore is named after the Malay word for Leatherback Turtle?

Pop Culture: Which 1979 film, adapted from Paul Theroux's novel of the same name and shot in Singapore, follows the seedy activities of American Jack Flowers, and was banned locally until 2006?

Sport: Malaya's victory in the 1949 Thomas Cup sparked the construction of which important sports venue in Guillemard Road?

History: What object, to be found in Empress Place, commemorates the 1850 visit to Singapore of the Marquis of Dalhousie, governor-general of India?

General Knowledge: The Beverley Mai, in Tomlinson Road, was the first example of what type of building when it opened in 1974?

Nature: What does the caterpillar of the Lime Butterfly look like?

Money and Power: Which is Singapore's oldest country club, founded in 1891?

Language: What is the English translation of the Eurasian Kristang phrase *'Bang pamiang'*?

Quiz 166

Arts and Literature: Which celebrated Singapore author, who died in 2002, penned *Moonrise, Sunset, Sayang* and *A Candle or the Sun*?

Food and Drink: Which Indian bread is traditionally baked in a tandoor (round oven)?

Geography: Which country became the newest member of ASEAN, joining in 1999?

Pop Culture: What was comic character Phua Chu Kang's favourite way to describe something that was the best?

Sport: On which road would you find the clubhouse of the Ceylon Sports Club, an organisation specialising in cricket and hockey?

History: What transportation first did Farrer Park host in 1919?

General Knowledge: Name the American teenager caned for vandalism in 1994?

Nature: What proportion of resident birds have become extinct in Singapore since 1819?

Money and Power: Which Singaporean politician was formerly chief executive officer of Singapore General Hospital from 2000 to 2001?

Language: What institution promotes French language and culture in Singapore?

Quiz 167

Arts and Literature: In which of Colin Cheong's novels does Timid Tim appear?

Food and Drink: What was the popular name for Cold Storage's Magnolia Snack Bars in the 1960s?

Geography: Which HDB new town has a name meaning 'end of the river'?

Pop Culture: *Fragments of the Same Dead Star* is the 2006 album release by which indie rock band?

Sport: Ong Poh Lim and Ismail Marjan formed a successful doubles partnership in the 1950s in which racket sport?

History: What form of Christianity did the London Missionary Society introduce to Singapore in 1807?

General Knowledge: Sweets and other tasty offerings are left out for which god on Chinese New Year's Eve, in the hope that he will make a favourable report on the household to the heavens?

Nature: Bred at the National University of Singapore, what are genetically modified Zebra Fish called?

Money and Power: Who stood against Ong Teng Cheong in the 1993 presidential election, receiving almost 42% of the votes?

Language: What does the acronym TPE stand for?

Quiz 168

Arts and Literature: Chia Choo Suan is famous for writing and directing for what medium?

Food and Drink: What is the key ingredient that gives *nasi lemak* its delicious taste?

Geography: How many islands make up Singapore?

Pop Culture: Which model, singer and actress won a *Her World* beauty contest at the age of sixteen, was the first local singer to play the Singapore Indoor Stadium and starred with Jackie Chan and Owen Wilson in the 2003 film *Shanghai Knights*?

Sport: During 1999 and 2000, which racehorse won the Singapore Airlines International Cup, Singapore Derby and Queen Elizabeth II Cup, earning S$4.5 million in race winnings throughout his career?

History: George D. Coleman's surveys of Singapore allowed the first detailed publication of what useful item in 1836?

General Knowledge: What was the name of the mythological creature that people were supposed to have scared away every Chinese New Year's Eve, using torches and fireworks, in the early days of the festivities?

Nature: When the GloFish, genetically modified by the National University of Singapore, doesn't glow, what can be deduced?

Money and Power: Which was the first US bank, then called International Banking Corporation (IBC), to open in Singapore in 1902?

Language: What does the acronym CHIJ stand for?

Quiz 169

Arts and Literature: What are *qing, sanxian, sheng* and *gehu*?

Food and Drink: Since 2002, what has already been used but is still drinkable?

Geography: Which island lies between the main island of Singapore and Sentosa and plays host to a container terminal?

Pop Culture: Which 2003 film, directed by Royston Tan, follows the lives of five local teenagers and was the first Singaporean film to be shown at the Venice International Film Festival?

Sport: Which sport is most commonly associated with the Padang?

History: What was the name given to women, brought to Singapore by the Japanese during World War II, to work in its military brothels?

General Knowledge: What must the groom give to the bride's family to gain entry to their residence on the morning of a traditional Chinese wedding?

Nature: Various species of popular individual trees are protected under a scheme by the National Parks Board. What are they called?

Money and Power: In each constituency what body organises grassroots activities and acts as a link between the government and the people?

Language: What does the acronym DBS stand for?

Quiz 170

Arts and Literature: The Er Woo Amateur Musical & Dramatic Association specialised in what kind of music?

Food and Drink: Where did the hawkers from Orchard Gluttons Square move to in 1979?

Geography: Name the former rickshaw station at the junction of Neil Road and Tanjong Pagar Road.

Pop Culture: Name Singapore's first cinema, opened by the Shaw Organisation in 1927.

Sport: Percy Pennefather was a Singapore international player in the 1950s and national coach in the 1960s for which team sport?

History: In which year did Singapore join the Commonwealth?

General Knowledge: In Chinese religion, what is the spirit of a dead person called that resides in another object, such as a spirit tablet or a medium?

Nature: What structure, near MacRitchie Reservoir, allows its visitors to see the forest canopy at close quarters?

Money and Power: What local government authority ran the urban areas of Singapore from 1951 to 1965?

Language: What does the acronym PSA stand for?

Quiz 171

Arts and Literature: When was the National Theatre Chinese Orchestra founded?

Food and Drink: Who sent the first nutmeg seeds to Singapore in 1819?

Geography: Which industrial region of western Singapore is named after a Malay word for 'voracious shark'?

Pop Culture: What was remarkable about the Cathay-Keris Films' production of *Buloh Perundu,* in 1953?

Sport: How many touches are allowed in *sepak takraw* before the ball must be returned to the opposition team's side of the net?

History: What was the name of the conflict between Malaysia and Indonesia, between 1963 and 1966, over the union of Malaya with Singapore, Sabah and Sarawak?

General Knowledge: What is the oldest church building, constructed in 1836, still in existence in Singapore?

Nature: How do Black-horned Locusts produce a noise to attract a mate?

Money and Power: What statutory board provides training to the Singapore Government's administrative staff?

Language: What does the acronym JTC stand for?

Celebrity Quiz

Khoo Swee Chiow

**Adventurer, Inspirational Speaker
and Author of *Journeys to the Ends of the Earth*
and *Singapore to Beijing on a Bike***

Arts and Literature: What is a *guzheng*?

Food and Drink: Which chain of supermarkets does NTUC run?

Geography: What is Malaysia's second-largest city?

Pop Culture: What was the first film to be made in Singapore, a Malay-language production, in 1933?

Sport: How many players are there in a *sepak takraw* team?

History: What was the common name for local agents of foreign firms, in use between the 1840s and the 1940s?

General Knowledge: What practice, based in Chinese religion, tries to gain help from supernatural forces to maximise one's good luck?

Nature: What insect makes a very loud whining, chainsaw-like noise?

Money and Power: Which property development company has grown into a major multinational empire under the guidance of Kwek Leng Beng?

Language: What does the acronym NETS stand for?

Celebrity Bonus Question: By what method did renowned adventurer Khoo Swee Chiow travel between Hanoi and Singapore in 2007–08?

Quiz 173

Arts and Literature: What was the Singapore Chinese Orchestra known as prior to 1992?

Food and Drink: Which edible commodity is the logo for the Orchard Road district?

Geography: What physical feature was created from the islands of Ayer Chawan, Ayer Merbau, Merlimau, Pesak, Pesak Kechil, Sakra and Seraya?

Pop Culture: In the 'golden age' of Singapore film production, from the 1940s to the 1970s, in what language were most films made?

Sport: What part of the body cannot be used when playing *sepak takraw*?

History: Which influential Chinese leader's birthday is celebrated on the twenty-seventh day of the eighth month of the Chinese agrarian calendar?

General Knowledge: At 61 m in height, the tallest artificial example of what festive item was erected on Mount Faber in 2005?

Nature: Which predatory insect can turn its head through 180 degrees?

Money and Power: Which parliamentary office holder administers the day-to-day running of parliament and its secretariat?

Language: What everyday communication tool goes by the prefixes 'cell' or 'mobile' in other parts of the world?

Quiz 174

Arts and Literature: *Huang Dao* (*Deserted Island*) was the literary supplement of which Singapore newspaper?

Food and Drink: Which Hokkien dish consists of a thin pastry skin surrounding a largely vegetarian filling?

Geography: What deepwater shelter dividing Singapore island from Sentosa and Pulau Brani was once known as New Harbour?

Pop Culture: Which 1998 film starred Adrian Pang as Hock, a grocer who wants to win a dance contest so that he can buy a motorbike?

Sport: Which sports club, established in 1852, is Singapore's second oldest and is located at the southern end of the Padang?

History: Name the programme of torture of civilians by the Japanese military police that began on 10 October 1943?

General Knowledge: What code of ethics, popular in the Chinese community, promotes such ideals as humanity, trustworthiness and filial piety?

Nature: What do the bright colours of the Painted Jezebel Butterfly mean?

Money and Power: Which is the highest court in Singapore?

Language: What is the English translation of the phrase *feng shui*?

Quiz 175

Arts and Literature: What kind of songs were Chinese choirs prohibited from singing?

Food and Drink: Traditionally, what other crop was pepper often grown with?

Geography: The only example left in Singapore of what formerly commonplace feature can be found at Lorong Buangkok?

Pop Culture: The 1940 film *Road to Singapore* starred which famous Hollywood double act?

Sport: What is *silat*?

History: Who was the Filipina maid executed for murdering her employer's 3-year-old son and another maid in 1995?

General Knowledge: What status can be lost in one of three ways: renunciation, cancellation or deprivation?

Nature: Which species of ant is often found in Singaporean homes?

Money and Power: The Common Effective Preferential Trade (CEPT) scheme operates between countries within which international organisation?

Language: What language was developed by the Eurasian community during the colonial era but has almost died out today?

Quiz 176

Arts and Literature: Which violinist heads the Jade Quartet and is also a long-serving member of the Singapore Symphony Orchestra?

Food and Drink: Which cooking method steams ingredients so that they remain full of flavour and lose very few nutrients?

Geography: Which shopping mall shares a block with the Swissôtel The Stamford and Raffles The Plaza hotels?

Pop Culture: Which actress starred in the television drama serials *Beautiful Connection* (2002) and *My Lucky Charm* (2005)?

Sport: What colour football strip does the Singapore national team wear?

History: What was Singapore's first Hindu temple, built in 1927, and located on South Bridge Road?

General Knowledge: Singapore Philatelic Museum occupies a building which used to be part of which famous school?

Nature: What is a White-rumped Shama?

Money and Power: Which company publishes most of Singapore's newspapers and also has interests in TV, radio and printing?

Language: What family of languages does Tamil belong to?

Quiz 177

Arts and Literature: Which Malay artist, poet and playwright won a Cultural Medallion in 1999 for his literature?

Food and Drink: What drink would you receive if you ordered a Horlick Dinosaur?

Geography: Which Singapore new town is built on the site of the former Peck San Theng Chinese Cemetery?

Pop Culture: In the Singapore magazine *BigO*, what does the title 'BigO' stand for?

Sport: Who was Singapore's first female track athletics gold-medal winner, taking the 400 metres at the 1974 Asian Games in Tehran?

History: What did the British East India Company and the Dutch colonial authorities do to the Johor-Riau Kingdom in 1824?

General Knowledge: Which cinema on Beach Road was demolished to make way for Shaw Towers?

Nature: Eighty-five percent of Singapore was covered by what in 1819?

Money and Power: In which branch of medicine did politician Dr Vivian Balakrishnan specialise?

Language: What does the acronym APEC stand for?

Quiz 178

Arts and Literature: Name the artistic expression of Chinese characters through ink painting.

Food and Drink: Which crop was once grown extensively on Sentosa?

Geography: Ang Mo Kio, Serangoon and Yio Chu Kang originally began as what kind of settlement?

Pop Culture: Which 1998 film, starring Ewan McGregor, reconstructs the events surrounding Nick Leeson's loss-making activities at the Singapore office of Barings Bank?

Sport: Siew Shaw Her won one Asian Games gold medal, six Southeast Asian Games gold medals and twenty Singapore national titles in which aquatic sport?

History: What was the name of the Singapore Chinese volunteer force, led by Lieutenant-Colonel John D. Dalley, during World War II?

General Knowledge: What headgear distinguishes Singapore's commandos from regular soldiers?

Nature: How long can a Giant Forest Ant grow?

Money and Power: By what name is the Singapore and Straits Aerated Water Company now known?

Language: What is the English translation of the Eurasian Kristang phrase 'Bos jah kumi?'?

Quiz 179

Arts and Literature: Which member of the Nanyang School art movement was sometimes known as the 'gibbon painter'?

Food and Drink: What colour is the Indian Muslim version of *mee goreng*?

Geography: Name the lighthouse that stands on the island of Pedra Branca.

Pop Culture: *Pain-Stained Morning* is the 1994 debut album by which band?

Sport: Who won three gold medals for tenpin bowling at the 2002 Asian Games in Busan?

History: What was established in 1877 to represent the interests of the Chinese community in the Straits Settlements and was dissolved just before World War II?

General Knowledge: The import and sale of what food was banned in 1992?

Nature: What do anchovies feed on?

Money and Power: In which year did Singapore and China establish formal diplomatic relations?

Language: What does the acronym SMRT stand for?

Quiz 180

Arts and Literature: What is the Singapore Broadcasting Corporation Chinese Orchestra now known as?

Food and Drink: On what snack has Old Chang Kee based its success?

Geography: Which district, west of the Kallang Basin, is named after the Malay words for 'village of the white-barked tree'?

Pop Culture: What 1940 film, based on a play by Somerset Maugham, is set in colonial Singapore and stars Bette Davis?

Sport: When was the sport of *sepak takraw* first played at the Asian Games?

History: The first version of what important document, stating how Singapore is governed, first came into effect on 4 February 1867?

General Knowledge: Which Catholic church features in its grounds a full-size reconstruction of the Stations of the Cross, modelled on those in Lourdes, France?

Nature: What do termites 'farm' to help them break down the plant material they eat?

Money and Power: Which branch of the British Civil Service administered Singapore from 1867 until it gained self-government in 1959?

Language: What term is used in Standard Singapore(an) English instead of redundancy?

Quiz 181

Arts and Literature: Which newspaper literary supplement of the 1920s was instrumental in developing local Singapore Chinese literature?

Food and Drink: Which Katong establishment made Singapore's first three-tier wedding cake in the 1920s?

Geography: Which district was named after the Malay words for 'water cart' as it was known for the bullock carts that carried water from the well at Ann Siang Hill?

Pop Culture: At which former amusement park, now the site of a shopping mall, would you have found the Flamingo Night Club?

Sport: Which motor racing event was held between 1961 and 1973 on Upper Thomson Road?

History: What was the name of British East India Company's main trading post in Southeast Asia prior to Singapore?

General Knowledge: What traditional weighing instrument is used to symbolise a 'balanced relationship' at Peranakan weddings?

Nature: Which butterfly is white with black spots?

Money and Power: Which digital electronic products company, founded by Sim Wong Hoo, was the first Singaporean business to be listed on the US NASDAQ stock exchange in 1992?

Language: What is the dialect spoken by members of the community from the northern part of Fujian province in mainland China?

Quiz 182

Arts and Literature: What term was used in the 1930s to describe Malayan and Singaporean Chinese literature?

Food and Drink: Which well-known Singapore dish is a salad of several ingredients and originated in Java?

Geography: Which island, well known for its turtles, has also gone by the names Goa Island, Peak Island and Pulau Tembakau?

Pop Culture: Which film studio made the 1961 film *Hang Jebat*, starring M. Amin and Nordin Ahmed?

Sport: Which additional sports facility was going to be part of the Singapore Indoor Stadium but was dropped from plans before construction began?

History: To which city was Singapore first linked by undersea telegraph cables in 1871?

General Knowledge: What kind of people would be members of the organisation Darul Arqam?

Nature: Which large black and yellow butterfly lives in the forest canopy?

Money and Power: After independence, in what year were the first Singapore dollars issued?

Language: What does the acronym SARS stand for?

Quiz 183

Arts and Literature: Since 1965 what has been described by the term *Xin huawen wenxue*?

Food and Drink: What kind of bread is used in a Roti John?

Geography: What is the maximum depth of water that can be reclaimed as land using current technology?

Pop Culture: Which actor starred in the 1956 award-winning film about the life of historical Malay hero Hang Tuah?

Sport: How many golf courses are there at the Singapore Island Country Club?

History: Which ongoing conflict between the ruling authorities and the Malayan Communist Party took place between 1948 and 1960?

General Knowledge: What is conveyed along the North Tunnel from Kranji to Changi?

Nature: Which insect has a thin brown body and stays very still to keep hidden?

Money and Power: The Development Bank of Singapore (DBS) began its life as part of which government statutory board?

Language: What does the acronym GDP stand for?

Quiz 184

Arts and Literature: Who founded the Singapore Classical Guitar Society in 1967?

Food and Drink: What does the letter 'C' refer to when you order a Kopi-C?

Geography: In which Malaysian state is Bahau, the village intended for resettling Chinese and Eurasian Catholics during the Japanese Occupation of Singapore in World War II?

Pop Culture: Which Malay pop group released its debut album, *Suara Dunia* (*Voice of the World*), in 2004 and was headed by Indonesian Dimas Santoso?

Sport: Who won bodybuilding gold medals at both the 2002 Southeast Asian Games and the 2005 Asian Games in the welterweight (75 kg) category?

History: Which Malaysian political party was Tunku Abdul Rahman president of for twenty years from 1951?

General Knowledge: Which church, at the foot of Fort Canning, was designed by George D Coleman?

Nature: What non-native species is now Singapore's most common bird?

Money and Power: Which politician served as Leader of the House from 1968 to 1984?

Language: In which script is the Malay-language newspaper *Utusan Melayu* written?

Quiz 185

Arts and Literature: When was the Chinese Opera Institute founded?

Food and Drink: In which Indian city was *roti prata* created?

Geography: In what sector has Singapore shown growth of 20% between the 1960s and the present day?

Pop Culture: First published in 1960, what is Singapore's best-selling magazine for women?

Sport: The Singapore Khalsa Association was established in 1931 as a sports club for which community?

History: Which office block, on the corner of Orchard Road and Cairnhill Road, was bombed in 1985?

General Knowledge: What scheme has been used since 1987 to counteract Singapore's falling fertility rate?

Nature: Which nature reserve is located on Singapore's southern coast?

Money and Power: What kind of research is conducted as DSO National Laboratories?

Language: What does the acronym HSBC stand for?

Quiz 186

Arts and Literature: Which Chinese opera has been held at Kiew Lee Tong Temple every year since 1944?

Food and Drink: Which large, round member of the cucumber family often has a white powdery coat?

Geography: Which popular recreational feature and nature haven originally went by the name Thomson Road Reservoir?

Pop Culture: Which 2002 film follows the lives of three boys struggling in the lowest stream of their school?

Sport: Neo Chwee Kok won four gold medals at the 1951 Asian Games in New Delhi in which aquatic sport?

History: The boardroom of which building was used by the Japanese to accept the British surrender on 15 February 1942?

General Knowledge: Which Muslim festival marks the end of the Haj pilgrimage to Mecca and is celebrated with the sacrifice of animals?

Nature: What plant does Lakawood come from?

Money and Power: What organisation is responsible for regulating the value of the Singapore dollar?

Language: What was the first Chinese-language daily newspaper to be published in Singapore in 1881?

Quiz 187

Arts and Literature: Chinese opera is often performed in what kind of outdoor venue?

Food and Drink: Which hot tea is served with condensed milk and ginger juice?

Geography: Which is the only country to have a greater population density than Singapore?

Pop Culture: Which actor, regularly seen in Mandarin Chinese-language television serials, has appeared in *Suo Nanyang* (*The Awakening*) (1984), *Bao Yu Kuang Hua* (*Angel of Vengeance*) (1993) and *Gan Gan Zuo Ge Kai Xin Ren* (*Don't Worry, Be Happy*) (1996-2003)?

Sport: Which sports club, situated at the northern end of the Padang, was established in 1883 by the Eurasian community?

History: Which Resident of Singapore, sacked by Sir Stamford Raffles in 1823, claimed he was the true founder of Singapore until the day he died?

General Knowledge: What races traditionally take place during the festival of Duan Wu Jie (Fifth Moon Festival)?

Nature: What prehistoric marine creature can sometimes be seen at Labrador Nature Reserve?

Money and Power: Which statutory board has the task of attracting foreign investment to Singapore and nurturing its business and industrial sectors?

Language: Which modified form of Arabic script can be used for writing the Malay language?

Quiz 188

Arts and Literature: Who wrote the nineteenth-century works *The Tale of Abdullah's Voyage* and *Abdullah's Story*?

Food and Drink: What drink would you receive if you ordered a Tak Kiu (literally 'kick ball' in Hokkien)?

Geography: Which was the first HDB estate to have five-room flats in a slab block?

Pop Culture: What elevated choreography was first officially allowed at Coyote Ugly, Devils Bar and 37 The Bar after midnight on 31 July 2003?

Sport: What aquatic activity is practised by the Chinese sports club located in Amber Road?

History: Who was the last Sultan of the Johor-Riau Kingdom from 1823 to 1824?

General Knowledge: Which Singapore school was founded in 1886 by Bishop William Fitzjames Oldham of the American Methodist Mission?

Nature: Agriculture and housing development were the chief causes of an 88% decline in which of Singapore's habitats, between 1819 and 1880?

Money and Power: Name the first local bank in Singapore.

Language: What does the acronym AWARE stand for?

Quiz 189

Arts and Literature: In what way are Chinese street operas different from those held indoors?

Food and Drink: What kind of spicy dip is normally served with satay?

Geography: Which well-known ethnic area lies to the north of Sungei Road?

Pop Culture: Who was the director of the 1961 Malay film classic *Hang Jebat*?

Sport: What international team sports tournament, hosted at the National Stadium, was cancelled in 2003 due to the SARS outbreak?

History: Name the American teenager caned for vandalism in 1994.

General Knowledge: What memorial to 150 years of Singapore's existence sits in front of the National Archives of Singapore in Canning Rise?

Nature: The toxin of fish-eating Cone Snails can be used to make what type of medicine?

Money and Power: What French word describes Singapore's role as a country that imports goods then re-exports them to other destinations?

Language: What does the acronym LTA stand for?

Quiz 190

Arts and Literature: Cai Bixia is a renowned actress, director and writer in what genre?

Food and Drink: What was the name of the temporary tea and coffee stalls that used to be set up around the vendor's pushcart?

Geography: Which street now lies on the site of Telok Ayer Basin?

Pop Culture: Which pop star has had major successes with the albums *Lonely Travel* (2003), *Gain* (2006) and *Embrace* (2007) and was voted Outstanding Young Person of the World in 2003?

Sport: Through which company is legal betting on sports results allowed?

History: James Puthucheary and Edwin Thumboo were among students accused of sedition in 1954 at which famous legal proceedings?

General Knowledge: Which disease can be caught from the bite of an Aedes mosquito and displays the symptoms of fever, rashes, headaches, nausea and diarrhoea?

Nature: What type of plant was Labrador Nature Reserve originally intended to protect?

Money and Power: Which annual meeting brings together leaders of all ASEAN countries plus China, Japan, South Korea, Australia, New Zealand and India to discuss issues of importance to the region?

Language: What does the acronym NRIC stand for?

Quiz 191

Arts and Literature: Which area of Singapore was host to many Chinese opera theatres in the late nineteenth and early twentieth centuries?

Food and Drink: What cocktail did Ngiam Tong Boon create in the early 1900s at Raffles Hotel?

Geography: In 1942 where did Japanese forces first set foot in Singapore?

Pop Culture: Which Singapore-born fashion designer has his own London boutique and was the official womenswear designer for the 2004 British Academy Film Awards?

Sport: What accolade does the Singapore Sports Council confer on individuals or teams who have achieved outstanding sporting performances?

History: Although Singapore was founded in 1819, in which year did the British East India Company gain full sovereignty from its previous Malay rulers?

General Knowledge: Which Muslim festival marks the end of fasting during the month of Ramadan and is celebrated with prayers and family gatherings?

Nature: Of which class of warm-blooded animal can sixty wild species be found in Singapore?

Money and Power: What is the approximate percentage of Singapore government revenue raised through personal and corporate tax?

Language: Which Chinese-language daily newspaper has the highest circulation in Singapore?

Quiz 192

Arts and Literature: Which Chinese opera group is well known for its performances of *A Costly Impulse*, once broadcast across China to 700 million viewers in 1993?

Food and Drink: Which of these spirits is not an ingredient in a Singapore Sling: gin, vodka, cherry brandy or Cointreau?

Geography: What construction links Marina South and Marina East?

Pop Culture: Which *xinyao* singer had a major hit in 1986 with 'Lian Zhi Qi' ('Love's Refuge')?

Sport: Which education institution, opened in 2004 and based in Woodlands, develops the talents of young sports men and women?

History: Which communications institution occupied much of the Fullerton Building from 1928 to 1995?

General Knowledge: Who might be regarded as Singapore's first expat resident?

Nature: Which large predator was hunted to extinction in Singapore in the 1930s?

Money and Power: What is the fund designed to augment the schooling of high-achieving children from low-income families?

Language: Which is the only indigenous language of Singapore's four official languages?

Quiz 193

Arts and Literature: Which visually impaired artist held the first solo exhibition by a Singaporean at the United Nations headquarters in New York in 2005?

Food and Drink: Essentially what type of vegetable is *cai xin*?

Geography: Which MRT line runs from Punggol to Harbourfront?

Pop Culture: What type of cinema was the largest of its kind in Asia and thrived at Jurong during the 1970s and early 1980s?

Sport: Which aquatic sports club is located in Tanjong Rhu Road?

History: What happened in Singapore five days after it became part of Malaysia?

General Knowledge: In which year was the EZ-Link card introduced?

Nature: What kind of mammal makes up one third of Singapore's mammal species?

Money and Power: Name the insurance scheme, linked to the Central Provident Fund (CPF), that provides coverage for the aged if they require long-term care.

Language: Which dialect of Malay is the one most commonly spoken in Singapore?

Quiz 194

Arts and Literature: What is the name of the traditional Malay theatre form most popular from the 1900s to the 1930s?

Food and Drink: Which now-defunct supermarket opened on the current site of The Paragon on Orchard Road in 1958?

Geography: Which district and MRT interchange at the eastern end of Orchard Road is named after the Indian words for 'laundry steps'?

Pop Culture: Which five-piece band released its debut album 'So Much More Inside' in 2003?

Sport: Which Malaysian state did Singapore's football team defeat 4–0 when it won the Malaysia Cup for the last time in 1994?

History: What mode of transport was replaced by buses in 1925?

General Knowledge: What must someone have in order to register a new car in Singapore?

Nature: The 400 species of Brachyura that live in and around Singapore are better known by what name?

Money and Power: What is the minimum interest rate for a Central Provident Fund Ordinary Account, as enshrined by the CPF Act?

Language: Which author made famous the term 'Singlish' in the books *Eh, Goondu!* (1983) and *Lagi Goondu!* (1986)?

Celebrity Quiz

Suchen Christine Lim
Singapore Literature Prize-winning author

Arts and Literature: Why were several Chinese theatre groups shut down by the government during the 1960s?

Food and Drink: In the dish *sup tulang*, what part of the mutton delicacy is eaten?

Geography: What road is carried across the Kallang River by the Merdeka Bridge?

Pop Culture: Which singer and female impersonator graced the Boom Boom Room night club with his presence throughout the 1990s and into the twenty-first century?

Sport: Where was the original racecourse of the Singapore Turf Club before it moved to Bukit Timah in 1933?

History: What was the name of the dockside warehouses found along the Singapore River, particularly at Boat Quay and Clarke Quay?

General Knowledge: In military terms, what kind of weapon is an FH 2000?

Nature: What does the Yellow House Bat feed on?

Money and Power: After what interval must a general election be held?

Language: What is the standard form of Malay that is used as the official language in Malaysia and Singapore?

Celebrity Bonus Question: What is the title of Suchen's Singapore Literature Prize-winning novel?

Quiz 196

Arts and Literature: Which Chinese theatre company frequently tour public housing estates with plays about social issues?

Food and Drink: Name the world's biggest producer of *popiah* wrappers, based in Senoko.

Geography: At 105 metres in height, which hill overlooks Keppel Harbour and Sentosa?

Pop Culture: Which Indian directed the most films ever in Singapore, notching up thirty productions between 1950 and 1960, including the 1958 horror film *Orang Minyak* (*Oily Man*)?

Sport: In which year did the Singapore Turf Club move to its current premises in Kranji?

History: Who was Singapore's second prime minister?

General Knowledge: By what dimension does the second floor of many shophouses typically overhang, creating a shaded walkway?

Nature: How do most bats find their way around in the dark?

Money and Power: Which office-holder has the responsibility to dissolve parliament prior to a general election?

Language: What is the Malay phrase for 'uniform pronunciation', adopted in Singapore in 1993, which is intended to make all forms of Malay across Southeast Asia sound the same?

Quiz 197

Arts and Literature: Who was founding conductor and musical director of the Singapore Symphony Orchestra from 1979 to 1986?

Food and Drink: What is the more commonly used Malay term for the hot drink 'pulled tea'?

Geography: What term do the Chinese use to refer to the Malay Peninsula and maritime Southeast Asia?

Pop Culture: Which acclaimed songwriter wrote the musical *Beauty World* and songs for the musical version of *Phua Chu Kang*?

Sport: In which year was the first S.League championship held?

History: Ngo Cheng Poh, Leong Chin Woo and Ang Boon Chai were the victims of which infamous crime in 1971?

General Knowledge: What is the arrangement called whereby foreign shipowners can register their vessels in Singapore?

Nature: What colour stripes does a Plantain Squirrel have down its sides?

Money and Power: What is the minimum voting age?

Language: Name Singapore's Malay-language daily newspaper.

Quiz 198

Arts and Literature: What medium does renowned artist Chua Ek Kay work in?

Food and Drink: Name the wet market located at the junction of Bukit Timah Road and Serangoon Road.

Geography: Which reservoir surrounds Singapore Zoo on three sides?

Pop Culture: Which popular actor starred in the television drama *Shang Cheng Ji* (*Wounded Tracks*) in 1994 and the film *Qi Yi Lu Cheng* (*What a Wonderful World*) in 1995?

Sport: Who were the inaugural winners of the S.League in 1996?

History: What did Singapore have twenty-six of between 1826 and 1959?

General Knowledge: In 2007 what was the threshold of monthly earnings that divided 'foreign workers' from 'foreign talent'?

Nature: Which rare, tree-dwelling mammal is about the size of a cat?

Money and Power: Which publication officially publishes the results of a general election?

Language: Name Singapore's Malay-language terrestrial TV station.

Quiz 199

Arts and Literature: Who wrote the book of poetry *Beyond Symbols* (1984)?

Food and Drink: What kind of pancake is stretched, flipped and folded before frying?

Geography: What do Changi Airport, East Coast Park, Marina South and Tuas have in common?

Pop Culture: Which singer enjoyed great success in Singapore, Taiwan and Hong Kong with the album *Yi Han* (*Unfortunate*) in 1996?

Sport: Which of the golf courses at the Singapore Island Country Club is regarded as a championship course?

History: In 1951, during the Emergency, which British High Commissioner was killed by the Malayan Communist Party?

General Knowledge: Which Hindu festival is associated with a plethora of illuminations?

Nature: Which creature is associated with Kusu Island?

Money and Power: What is Singapore's oldest law firm, founded in 1874 by two English lawyers and currently based in Clifford Centre?

Language: Which is the largest Chinese dialect community in Singapore?

Quiz 200

Arts and Literature: In which visual art form is Chua Soo Bin an important and much-decorated exponent?

Food and Drink: Why are wet markets so named?

Geography: What 'flat field' has Singapore Recreation Club at one end and Singapore Cricket Club at the other?

Pop Culture: Which twins were leading lights of the 1980s *xinyao* music scene, one of them founding a school of music in his own name?

Sport: S.League footballers Lutz Pfannenstiel and Mirko Jurilj were found guilty of and banned for what offence in 2000?

History: Who was the Dutch girl over whom a high profile custody battle was fought in 1950 between her parents and a Malay friend, culminating in serious race riots?

General Knowledge: What kind of pass must a 'foreign worker' have?

Nature: The Palm Civet is active at what time of day?

Money and Power: Which organisation is responsible for keeping the register of voters up to date?

Language: Name the organisation that promotes the Malay language in Singapore.

Answers

Quiz 1
Arts and Literature: Action Theatre
Food and Drink: Asia Pacific Breweries
Geography: Adelphi Hotel
Pop Culture: Alhambra
Sport: Bodybuilding
History: The Battle of Pasir Panjang
General Knowledge: Abdul Gaffoor Mosque
Nature: Pitcher plant
Money and Power: Tunku Abdul Rahman
Language: Association of Southeast Asian Nations

Quiz 2
Arts and Literature: Agni Kootthu
Food and Drink: Root
Geography: Batam
Pop Culture: *Bujang Lapak*
Sport: Congkak
History: Storing ammunition
General Knowledge: Cash, car, credit card, condominium, country club
Nature: Pulau Ubin
Money and Power: Abdullah Tarmugi
Language: Bilingualism

Quiz 3
Arts and Literature: 2002
Food and Drink: Red
Geography: 6 kilometres
Pop Culture: Topless dance shows
Sport: Tan Tiang Boon
History: Kempeitai
General Knowledge: Jamae Mosque
Nature: Alpha male
Money and Power: They are all government-linked companies (GLCs)
Language: 'Alamak!'

Quiz 4
Arts and Literature: Glen Goei

Food and Drink: Braising
Geography: The sea
Pop Culture: Chu Beng
Sport: Grace Young
History: Israeli President Chaim Herzog
General Knowledge: MacDonald House
Nature: Military live firing
Money and Power: 20%
Language: Tamil

Quiz 5

Arts and Literature: W!LD RICE
Food and Drink: Tamarind
Geography: Nanyang Technological University
Pop Culture: Papa Rock
Sport: Sportswoman of the Year
History: 2000 BC
General Knowledge: 15 (Woodleigh is not currently operational)
Nature: Reticulated Python
Money and Power: Subordinate Courts
Language: Teochew

Quiz 6

Arts and Literature: Hear themselves playing
Food and Drink: Guangdong
Geography: Coleman Bridge
Pop Culture: October Cherries
Sport: Lloyd Valberg
History: John Laycock
General Knowledge: Jehovah's Witnesses
Nature: 40%
Money and Power: Sijori Growth Triangle
Language: 'Bo chap'

Quiz 7

Arts and Literature: They are hearing impaired
Food and Drink: Pandan
Geography: Lower Seletar Reservoir
Pop Culture: The Siglap Five
Sport: The owner
History: Merdeka talks
General Knowledge: Anglo-Chinese School

Nature: Green
Money and Power: Law Society of Singapore
Language: Double confirm

Quiz 8
Arts and Literature: Nanyang Style
Food and Drink: Lime
Geography: Little India
Pop Culture: Tropicana
Sport: Toa Payoh Stadium
History: Outram Prison
General Knowledge: 20 years
Nature: Fish
Money and Power: Central Provident Fund (CPF)
Language: Their English is not good

Quiz 9
Arts and Literature: Frontier Danceland
Food and Drink: *Kangkong*
Geography: Hong Lim Park
Pop Culture: Douglas Oliveiro
Sport: Basketball
History: The Labour Party
General Knowledge: 600 grammes
Nature: Plant kingdom
Money and Power: Hotel Properties Limited (HPL)
Language: *Sotong* (squid)

Celebrity Quiz—Nancy Lam
Arts and Literature: Getai
Food and Drink: Ladies' fingers
Geography: Strait of Malacca
Pop Culture: Orchard Cinema
Sport: James Wong
History: Tanjong Pagar
General Knowledge: Keramat
Nature: Bukit Timah Expressway (BKE)
Money and Power: Household
Language: Understand Singlish
Celebrity Bonus Question: Yummy Yummy

Quiz 11

Arts and Literature: Ghazal
Food and Drink: Eggs
Geography: Suez Canal
Pop Culture: The Padres
Sport: Wong Peng Soon
History: 1948
General Knowledge: Killer litter
Nature: It is found nowhere else in the world
Money and Power: Hong Kong & Shanghai Banking Corporation (HSBC)
Language: TalkingCock.com

Quiz 12

Arts and Literature: Carl Gibson-Hill
Food and Drink: *Kai lan* (Chinese kale)
Geography: Johor
Pop Culture: P Ramlee
Sport: Joscelin Yeo
History: Lim Bo Seng
General Knowledge: Valuair
Nature: Nature Society (Singapore), or NSS
Money and Power: Hyflux
Language: *Coxford Singlish Dictionary*

Quiz 13

Arts and Literature: Ahmad Jaafar
Food and Drink: Bengawan Solo
Geography: Riau Islands
Pop Culture: Capitol Theatre
Sport: Golf
History: Abu Bakar
General Knowledge: Badang
Nature: Forest
Money and Power: ABN AMRO
Language: English

Quiz 14

Arts and Literature: Durian fruit
Food and Drink: Cream crackers
Geography: Roads
Pop Culture: The Observatory

Sport: Two
History: Lai Teck
General Knowledge: Japanese
Nature: They have no natural predators
Money and Power: Gross Domestic Product (GDP)
Language: Kiasu

Quiz 15

Arts and Literature: Goethe Institute
Food and Drink: Vermicelli
Geography: Telok Ayer Bay
Pop Culture: B N Rao
Sport: Squash
History: Majapahit
General Knowledge: Synagogue
Nature: Giant Tree Squirrel
Money and Power: India
Language: Singapore

Quiz 16

Arts and Literature: Classical music
Food and Drink: Beef
Geography: Strait of Johor
Pop Culture: Rahimah Rahim
Sport: Table tennis
History: Malayan People's Anti-Japanese Army (MPAJA)
General Knowledge: Nine
Nature: Tiger Orchid
Money and Power: Japan
Language: Hokkien

Quiz 17

Arts and Literature: Piano
Food and Drink: Coconut milk
Geography: Woodlands
Pop Culture: S K Poon
Sport: Doha, Qatar 2006
History: Kampung Temenggung
General Knowledge: Maintenance of Religious Harmony Act
Nature: A fish
Money and Power: Institute of Policy Studies
Language: Nanyang Technological University (NTU)

Quiz 18
Arts and Literature: Tamil
Food and Drink: Cockles
Geography: Bintan
Pop Culture: Rita Chao
Sport: *Gasing*
History: Joshua Chiu Ban It
General Knowledge: The American Club
Nature: 1951
Money and Power: 13th month bonus
Language: Cantonese

Quiz 19
Arts and Literature: Goh Poh Seng
Food and Drink: It is cooked until it almost dries up
Geography: Yishun
Pop Culture: The Quests
Sport: Shooting
History: Malayan Airlines
General Knowledge: Marina Barrage
Nature: The Vanda Miss Joaquim Orchid
Money and Power: The Istana
Language: Tamil drum

Quiz 20
Arts and Literature: Toy Factory Theatre Ensemble
Food and Drink: Dark soy sauce
Geography: Tuas Second Link
Pop Culture: *Return to Pontianak*
Sport: Asian Games
History: Malacca Sultanate
General Knowledge: Maid
Nature: A fish
Money and Power: Infocomm Development Authority of Singapore (IDA)
Language: Sri Mariamman Temple

Quiz 21
Arts and Literature: Naa Govindasamy
Food and Drink: Herbs
Geography: Choa Chu Kang
Pop Culture: B S Rajhans

Sport: Three
History: Malayan Democratic Union (MDU)
General Knowledge: MATADOR
Nature: Hybrid orchid
Money and Power: J. B. Jeyaretnam
Language: English and Malay

Quiz 22

Arts and Literature: Lan Shui
Food and Drink: White
Geography: Factories
Pop Culture: *Goal*
Sport: Delta Sports Complex
History: Nicoll Highway collapse
General Knowledge: India
Nature: At night
Money and Power: Mace
Language: It is not very difficult ('a little drop of water')

Quiz 23

Arts and Literature: *Ah Kong's Birthday Party*
Food and Drink: Crab
Geography: Jurong Lake
Pop Culture: Pop Ye Ye
Sport: Swimming
History: Malayan Union
General Knowledge: Expo
Nature: Spider Orchid
Money and Power: They are only appointed for a fixed term, not permanently
Language: Channel U

Quiz 24

Arts and Literature: Alfian Sa'at
Food and Drink: *Bak chor mee*
Geography: Lot's Wife
Pop Culture: Bionic Boy
Sport: Shooting
History: Aljunied
General Knowledge: Battle Box
Nature: Fern
Money and Power: Administrative Service

Language: Two

Quiz 25

Arts and Literature: Three (main, side and rear)
Food and Drink: Goat
Geography: Sengkang
Pop Culture: The Surfers
Sport: Badminton
History: *Laju*
General Knowledge: S$500
Nature: 70%
Money and Power: Gross National Income (GNI)
Language: He's a playboy

Quiz 26

Arts and Literature: Ho Minfang
Food and Drink: Tamarind and coriander
Geography: Dover Road
Pop Culture: Rex
Sport: Swimming
History: Two months
General Knowledge: They become opaque when passing through residential areas to maintain the privacy of the locals.
Nature: Raffles Collection
Money and Power: Khoo Teck Puat
Language: World Intellectual Property Organisation

Quiz 27

Arts and Literature: Dance
Food and Drink: When it is unripe
Geography: Ayer Rajah Expressway (AYE)
Pop Culture: *Ring of Fury*
Sport: 2000
History: They were the landing sites for the Japanese invasion of Malaya
General Knowledge: Light Rail Transit (LRT) system
Nature: Red Junglefowl
Money and Power: Knowledge-based economy
Language: Military

Quiz 28

Arts and Literature: Indian classical music

Food and Drink: Sweetness
Geography: Pedra Branca
Pop Culture: Sakura
Sport: Sand
History: 130,000
General Knowledge: Dhoby Ghaut
Nature: A snake
Money and Power: McDonalds
Language: 'Berak'

Quiz 29
Arts and Literature: Indian classical music
Food and Drink: Portuguese
Geography: VivoCity
Pop Culture: Yodelling
Sport: Singapore Airlines International Cup
History: David Marshall
General Knowledge: Stamford Canal
Nature: Rainforest
Money and Power: Tripartism
Language: 'Chin chye, lah!'

Quiz 30
Arts and Literature: People's Association
Food and Drink: Banana sauce
Geography: Sentosa
Pop Culture: Anita Sarawak
Sport: 2,000 metres
History: Marxist conspiracy
General Knowledge: Merdeka Bridge
Nature: Buried in the mud
Money and Power: Shipping
Language: A 'chio bu' is an attractive woman

Celebrity Quiz—Lee Wei Song
Arts and Literature: Pottery
Food and Drink: *Payasam*
Geography: Sembawang
Pop Culture: 'Can't Buy Me Love'
Sport: July
History: The introduction of National Service
General Knowledge: Merlion

Nature: It can live in salt water
Money and Power: High Court judge
Language: Sense of smell
Celebrity Bonus Question: To develop new artistes for Chinese markets
worldwide.

Quiz 32

Arts and Literature: The pipe organ
Food and Drink: *Lohan chai*
Geography: Read Bridge
Pop Culture: The Oddfellows
Sport: Water polo
History: Lee Hsien Loong
General Knowledge: Junior college
Nature: Amphibian
Money and Power: Underwater World
Language: Clever (streetwise)

Quiz 33

Arts and Literature: Madhatters Comedy Company
Food and Drink: Sago
Geography: Kranji
Pop Culture: Singapore Girl
Sport: November
History: British colonial rule
General Knowledge: Millennia Institute
Nature: Northern Peninsular Malaysia
Money and Power: Stockbroking
Language: Alcohol

Quiz 34

Arts and Literature: Philip Jeyaretnam
Food and Drink: Gingko nuts
Geography: Tampines Expressway (TPE)
Pop Culture: Silver Screen Awards
Sport: 2005
History: Merlion
General Knowledge: Handphone
Nature: By gliding
Money and Power: Lee & Lee
Language: Eye power

Quiz 35

Arts and Literature: *Empat* (*Four*)
Food and Drink: Boat Quay
Geography: Bedok
Pop Culture: Cathay-Keris Films
Sport: Dragon boat races
History: Yemen
General Knowledge: Benjamin Sheares Bridge
Nature: Long-tailed macaque
Money and Power: Ahmad Ibrahim
Language: Two

Quiz 36

Arts and Literature: Dance
Food and Drink: Translucent
Geography: Mandai Road
Pop Culture: Fashion design
Sport: The American Club
History: Methodists
General Knowledge: 1985
Nature: 1859
Money and Power: Mathematics
Language: Run the country (it means government)

Quiz 37

Arts and Literature: Jubilee Hall
Food and Drink: Dessert
Geography: Choa Chu Kang
Pop Culture: The Stylers
Sport: 1965
History: SilkAir crash
General Knowledge: Mount Alvernia
Nature: Herbarium
Money and Power: Teck Ghee
Language: Failure

Quiz 38

Arts and Literature: Kallang Theatre
Food and Drink: Wheat
Geography: Pasir Ris
Pop Culture: Stefanie Sun
Sport: Victor's Superbowl

History: Police station
General Knowledge: Myopia
Nature: 1995
Money and Power: Minister for Trade & Industry
Language: None

Quiz 39
Arts and Literature: Violin
Food and Drink: Green
Geography: Pan-Island Expressway (PIE) and East Coast Parkway (ECP)
Pop Culture: Stefanie Sun
Sport: Singapore Masters
History: Drug trafficking
General Knowledge: Zubir Said
Nature: Evolution Garden
Money and Power: Ang Mo Kio
Language: *Jia lat*

Quiz 40
Arts and Literature: Tamil
Food and Drink: Sweetness
Geography: Simei
Pop Culture: The Swallows
Sport: Ang Peng Siong
History: Omar Kampung Melaka Mosque
General Knowledge: The Old Ford Motor Factory
Nature: Fighting Spider
Money and Power: Lee Hsien Yang
Language: Past (it means 'already')

Quiz 41
Arts and Literature: Malay poetry
Food and Drink: Mill (mangle)
Geography: Sungei Bedok
Pop Culture: Sylvester Sim
Sport: Home United
History: Sook Ching
General Knowledge: Singapore Ear
Nature: It does not live in urban areas
Money and Power: Derivatives
Language: Sanskrit

Quiz 42

Arts and Literature: Joyce Koh
Food and Drink: Dried slices
Geography: Ang Mo Kio
Pop Culture: Royston Tan
Sport: Tao Li
History: Vehicle license plate
General Knowledge: Order of Temasek
Nature: It vibrates to become blurred and difficult to see
Money and Power: Tanjong Pagar
Language: Own Time Own Target

Quiz 43

Arts and Literature: Drum
Food and Drink: Soya milk
Geography: Serangoon
Pop Culture: Zoe Tay
Sport: Chua Phung Kim
History: Car
General Knowledge: Crescent moon
Nature: St Andrew's Cross Spider
Money and Power: Six
Language: It's a fierce and arrogant woman

Quiz 44

Arts and Literature: Stella Kon
Food and Drink: Seasoning
Geography: Kallang River
Pop Culture: Tea dances
Sport: Gombak Stadium
History: Blue and white Chinese porcelain
General Knowledge: National Kidney Foundation
Nature: On their mother's back
Money and Power: Nick Leeson
Language: Flatter them

Quiz 45

Arts and Literature: P. Krishnan
Food and Drink: Green mung bean
Geography: Braddell Road
Pop Culture: SARS TV
Sport: Singapore Allcomers Record

History: Hotel de L'Europe
General Knowledge: Raffles Museum
Nature: It dives into the water and drags them on land
Money and Power: Lim Swee Say
Language: Punjabi

Quiz 46

Arts and Literature: The Stage Club
Food and Drink: BreadTalk
Geography: Woodleigh
Pop Culture: Rose Chan
Sport: Lionel Lewis
History: Sunny Ang
General Knowledge: The proportion of the population of Chinese descent
Nature: Amphibian
Money and Power: Property investment
Language: British Council

Quiz 47

Arts and Literature: Kuo Pao Kun
Food and Drink: Sourness
Geography: Mount Alvernia Hospital
Pop Culture: Channel 8
Sport: Hammer
History: S. R. Nathan
General Knowledge: Operationally Ready National Serviceman (ORNS)
Nature: Golden Web Spider
Money and Power: Low Thia Kiang
Language: Boredom

Quiz 48

Arts and Literature: Chinese opera
Food and Drink: Blue
Geography: Temasek Polytechnic
Pop Culture: *He Lan Cun (Holland Village)*
Sport: Cuesports Singapore
History: *God Save the Queen*
General Knowledge: Individual Physical Proficiency Test (IPPT)
Nature: In the webs of other spiders
Money and Power: Lucky Plaza
Language: Suaku

Quiz 49

Arts and Literature: Sculpture
Food and Drink: Pepper
Geography: Bukit Batok Town Park
Pop Culture: Shaw Brothers
Sport: 1993
History: Malayan Forum
General Knowledge: North South Line
Nature: Bamboo Orchid
Money and Power: Puisne judge
Language: Mandarin Chinese and Tamil

Quiz 50

Arts and Literature: LaSalle–SIA College of the Arts
Food and Drink: They should be soaked in water
Geography: MacPherson
Pop Culture: *Sandiwara*
Sport: East Coast Park
History: 1993
General Knowledge: New Creation Church
Nature: Siberia
Money and Power: Mah Bow Tan
Language: 'Tebalek'

Quiz 51

Arts and Literature: Lee Hock Mah
Food and Drink: Square
Geography: New Upper Changi Road
Pop Culture: 1960s
Sport: Choa Chu Kang
History: Operation Cold Store
General Knowledge: Nicoll Highway collapse
Nature: September to April
Money and Power: Malayan Motors
Language: Off the beaten track (remote)

Quiz 52

Arts and Literature: 5 years old
Food and Drink: Liquorice
Geography: Eunos Industrial Estate
Pop Culture: Police
Sport: Jurong

History: Operation Jaywick
General Knowledge: Red
Nature: 1993
Money and Power: MediFund
Language: S

Quiz 53
Arts and Literature: Gerrie Lim
Food and Drink: *Bak kut teh*
Geography: Fort Canning
Pop Culture: New World
Sport: Ang Peng Siong
History: Alexandra Hospital
General Knowledge: Doctor
Nature: Black-spotted Sticky Frog
Money and Power: Union Bank of Calcutta
Language: 'I can accept a lesser alternative' (a direct translation of the Hokkien idiom '*Bo hir hay mah hoh*')

Quiz 54
Arts and Literature: Lee Wen
Food and Drink: The wings
Geography: Geylang Road
Pop Culture: Maggie Teng
Sport: Albirex Niigata
History: The recapture of Singapore
General Knowledge: one-north
Nature: Over 50 years old
Money and Power: Nominated Member of Parliament (NMP)
Language: It's a handsome man

Quiz 55
Arts and Literature: Maria Menado
Food and Drink: Mushroom
Geography: Cuppage Terrace
Pop Culture: Lydia Lum
Sport: Jalan Besar Stadium
History: The ship sank
General Knowledge: Qi Qiao Jie
Nature: Emerald Dove
Money and Power: Oversea-Chinese Banking Corporation (OCBC)
Language: Post Office Savings Bank

Quiz 56

Arts and Literature: Yangqin (Chinese dulcimer)
Food and Drink: Galangal
Geography: Marine Parade
Pop Culture: The Thunderbirds
Sport: Balestier Khalsa
History: Orang Laut
General Knowledge: Pulau Ubin
Nature: It is a hybrid species
Money and Power: Ministry of Defence (MINDEF)
Language: Don't go back on your word

Quiz 57

Arts and Literature: Christopher Allen
Food and Drink: Radish
Geography: Tanjung Pinang
Pop Culture: Python
Sport: Fandi Ahmad
History: Anglicanism
General Knowledge: Alexandra Barracks
Nature: Bukit Timah Nature Reserve
Money and Power: American Chamber of Commerce
Language: Mandarin Chinese

Celebrity Quiz—Ho Yeow Sun

Arts and Literature: Suchen Christine Lim
Food and Drink: Soaking in warm water
Geography: Dunearn Road
Pop Culture: Kelvin Tong
Sport: Balestier Central
History: Cemeteries
General Knowledge: Zoroastrianism
Nature: Rose and Violet
Money and Power: Malaysia
Language: 'Last time policeman wear shorts!'
Celebrity Bonus Question: Wyclef Jean

Quiz 59

Arts and Literature: Stage floor
Food and Drink: Chinese New Year
Geography: Sisters' Islands
Pop Culture: Odeon

Sport: Tenpin bowling
History: Raffles Institution
General Knowledge: Jurong BirdPark
Nature: Reptile
Money and Power: Ho Ching
Language: They would be a busybody

Quiz 60

Arts and Literature: Lim Tze Peng
Food and Drink: Black
Geography: Rochor Canal
Pop Culture: *12 Storeys*
Sport: Bedok Stadium
History: India
General Knowledge: Paya Lebar Airport
Nature: Indonesia
Money and Power: Mustaq Ahmad
Language: Manglish

Quiz 61

Arts and Literature: Lim Yau
Food and Drink: Fertility
Geography: Revenue House
Pop Culture: Wang Sa
Sport: The Eagles
History: Straits Settlements
General Knowledge: Namibia
Nature: White
Money and Power: Mufti
Language: Diglossia

Quiz 62

Arts and Literature: J. M. Sali
Food and Drink: Century egg
Geography: Horse racing
Pop Culture: A-Do
Sport: President's Cup
History: *Spyros*
General Knowledge: Athlete's foot
Nature: Black-naped Oriole
Money and Power: Singapore Management University
Language: Arabic

Quiz 63
Arts and Literature: Liu Beian
Food and Drink: Sour
Geography: Nassim Road
Pop Culture: Chris
Sport: The Protectors
History: Lieutenant-General Arthur Percival
General Knowledge: Pentecostal
Nature: Lesser Tree Duck
Money and Power: None
Language: East Coast (because of its association with British civil servants and Singapore's wealthy)

Quiz 64
Arts and Literature: Jazz
Food and Drink: Spring roll
Geography: Tanglin Road
Pop Culture: Phua Chu Kang
Sport: Police
History: Raffles Hotel
General Knowledge: Mount Faber
Nature: Because it is being captured to meet demand by songbird fanciers
Money and Power: Two-thirds
Language: Sarong Party Girl

Quiz 65
Arts and Literature: Nanyang Style
Food and Drink: Thai Jasmine rice
Geography: Raffles Town Club
Pop Culture: X-Periment
Sport: Ministry of Home Affairs
History: Yusof Ishak
General Knowledge: 'Very hazardous'
Nature: Brahminy Kite
Money and Power: National Trades Union Congress (NTUC)
Language: They are repeated (e.g. don't pray-pray)

Quiz 66
Arts and Literature: Earl Lu
Food and Drink: Basmati rice
Geography: Holland Village

Pop Culture: *I Not Stupid*
Sport: Yishun Stadium
History: Force Z
General Knowledge: 1966
Nature: White-bellied Sea Eagle
Money and Power: Tata Steel
Language: 'Kena'

Quiz 67
Arts and Literature: Madhavi Krishnan
Food and Drink: *Ketupat*
Geography: Ulu Pandan Road
Pop Culture: The Crazy Bumpkins
Sport: Queenstown Stadium
History: Mission Press
General Knowledge: The Old Ford Motor Factory
Nature: Grey
Money and Power: Neptune Orient Lines (NOL)
Language: Particle

Quiz 68
Arts and Literature: Goh Choo San
Food and Drink: They should be lightly cracked
Geography: Tampines
Pop Culture: The Beatles
Sport: Weightlifting
History: Federation of Malaya
General Knowledge: Malaria
Nature: A fish
Money and Power: Integrated resort
Language: Tamil

Quiz 69
Arts and Literature: Malay Language Council of Singapore
Food and Drink: It makes it darker
Geography: Beach Road
Pop Culture: Zhuang Xuefang
Sport: Hougang Stadium
History: Race riots
General Knowledge: Six
Nature: White-breasted Waterhen
Money and Power: Ng Teng Fong

Language: Lah

Quiz 70
Arts and Literature: Singapore Association of Writers
Food and Drink: Wasabi
Geography: Average life expectancy at birth
Pop Culture: Ten
Sport: Aide Iskandar
History: Tangs
General Knowledge: An ammunition dump
Nature: Black
Money and Power: Tangs
Language: Mulligatawny

Quiz 71
Arts and Literature: Indonesia
Food and Drink: *Chinchalok*
Geography: Marina Square
Pop Culture: ZoukOut
Sport: Choa Chu Kang Stadium
History: Sophia
General Knowledge: Fifteen
Nature: Egg collecting
Money and Power: Insurance
Language: Surprise

Quiz 72
Arts and Literature: Singapore Symphony Orchestra
Food and Drink: Cinnamon
Geography: Bedok Jetty
Pop Culture: Cleopatra Wong
Sport: Jurong East Stadium
History: Opium
General Knowledge: Opium
Nature: Monitor lizard
Money and Power: 21 years old
Language: They are turning it on

Quiz 73
Arts and Literature: Masuri S. N.
Food and Drink: Thick dark soy sauce
Geography: Raffles Hotel

Pop Culture: *The Champion*
Sport: Stag
History: Java
General Knowledge: Christmas
Nature: It does not migrate
Money and Power: Christina Ong
Language: Central Narcotics Bureau

Quiz 74
Arts and Literature: Sculpture
Food and Drink: *Mee pok*
Geography: Rendezvous Hotel
Pop Culture: Moses Lim
Sport: Young Lions
History: Three
General Knowledge: Forty-five
Nature: Its legs
Money and Power: OSIM
Language: Operationally Ready Date

Celebrity Quiz—Benny Ong
Arts and Literature: W. Somerset Maugham
Food and Drink: Turmeric
Geography: Singapore Management University (SMU)
Pop Culture: *Return of the Condor Heroes*
Sport: Twice
History: Malay
General Knowledge: They are all secular public holidays
Nature: A bird
Money and Power: Ong Teng Cheong
Language: Media Development Authority
Celebrity Bonus Question: Lady Diana

Quiz 76
Arts and Literature: Teater Ekamatra
Food and Drink: *Hae koh*
Geography: Chijmes
Pop Culture: TVMobile
Sport: Wolf
History: Sir Stamford Raffles
General Knowledge: Eleven
Nature: By lifting its food from the water during flight

Money and Power: Ocean Garments
Language: 'Then you know.'

Quiz 77
Arts and Literature: Ministry of Information, Communications and the Arts
Food and Drink: Glutinous rice
Geography: Midpoint Orchard
Pop Culture: Dim sum killer
Sport: Singapore Armed Forces FC
History: None
General Knowledge: The deceased
Nature: Green
Money and Power: Pan-Electric Industries Ltd
Language: Public Utilities Board

Quiz 78
Arts and Literature: Modern Art Society
Food and Drink: Rice wine
Geography: Orchard Towers
Pop Culture: Fish balls
Sport: Sinchi
History: National University of Singapore (NUS)
General Knowledge: Down a well
Nature: The back of its neck
Money and Power: An Act
Language: Raffles Junior College

Quiz 79
Arts and Literature: Photography
Food and Drink: For medicinal and dental purposes
Geography: Straits of Singapore
Pop Culture: The Checkmates
Sport: To see whose top spins the longest
History: Anglo-Dutch Treaty
General Knowledge: The Anglican Church
Nature: Four
Money and Power: Baht
Language: Certificate of Entitlement

Quiz 80
Arts and Literature: Chinese opera

Food and Drink: Medium-grain white rice
Geography: Singapore Botanic Gardens
Pop Culture: X'Ho
Sport: Bishan Stadium
History: Suma Oriental
General Knowledge: 60.5 kg
Nature: By soaring around it on heat thermals
Money and Power: United States of America
Language: Mandarin Chinese

Quiz 81

Arts and Literature: Muhammad Ariff Ahmad (MAS)
Food and Drink: *Gado gado*
Geography: Gleneagles Hospital
Pop Culture: *Maggi & Me*
Sport: Mirko Grabovac
History: Charlie Chaplin
General Knowledge: Raffles Lighthouse
Nature: Head down
Money and Power: 15 April
Language: Singapore Symphony Orchestra

Quiz 82

Arts and Literature: Museum, NUS Centre for the Arts
Food and Drink: Samosa
Geography: Lau Pa Sat
Pop Culture: *Deal or No Deal*
Sport: SingTel League Cup
History: Robinsons
General Knowledge: Raffles Institution
Nature: In tree holes
Money and Power: Philips
Language: Trans-Island Bus Services

Quiz 83

Arts and Literature: Singapore International Film Festival
Food and Drink: Rambutan
Geography: The same time zone
Pop Culture: Olinda Cho
Sport: Vietnam
History: Sir Shenton Thomas
General Knowledge: Thaipusam

Nature: Leopard Cat
Money and Power: Singapore Pools
Language: Blindness

Quiz 84
Arts and Literature: Nasyid
Food and Drink: *Char siew*
Geography: Pearl's Hill
Pop Culture: Guo Yao Yao
Sport: 11–0
History: Samsui women
General Knowledge: They are Republic of Singapore Air Force bases
Nature: Indian cuckoo
Money and Power: PSA International
Language: Singapore

Quiz 85
Arts and Literature: Tan Hian Por
Food and Drink: Red chilli
Geography: Selat Jurong
Pop Culture: Sim Lim Square
Sport: In a pyramid
History: Lieutenant-General Yamashita Tomoyuki
General Knowledge: Javanese
Nature: Asian Toad
Money and Power: Sylvia Lim
Language: Republic of Singapore Navy

Quiz 86
Arts and Literature: National Library
Food and Drink: Pig's organ soup
Geography: Bukit Gombak
Pop Culture: Tay Ping Hui
Sport: 9–0
History: Scouts
General Knowledge: Two (Tuas and Changi)
Nature: Plaintive Cuckoo
Money and Power: S. Rajaratnam
Language: American Sign Language

Quiz 87
Arts and Literature: It was demolished

Food and Drink: Flour
Geography: Kovan
Pop Culture: Ivy Lee
Sport: Malik Awab
History: Secret society
General Knowledge: Woodlands
Nature: Hoot
Money and Power: Recession
Language: Sino-Tibetan

Quiz 88

Arts and Literature: Ornamental stonework
Food and Drink: Seaweed
Geography: Aljunied
Pop Culture: Channel 8
Sport: Fandi Ahmad
History: *Sejarah Melayu* (*Malay Annals*)
General Knowledge: Restroom Association (Singapore)
Nature: In a small depression in the ground
Money and Power: Paula Abdul
Language: Putonghua

Quiz 89

Arts and Literature: Ong Keng San
Food and Drink: *Kueh lapis*
Geography: Redhill
Pop Culture: Joanne Peh
Sport: Iraq
History: German
General Knowledge: Road Tax
Nature: Mangroves
Money and Power: Second wing policy
Language: Beijing dialect

Quiz 90

Arts and Literature: Dance
Food and Drink: Hainan
Geography: Tanah Merah
Pop Culture: Edmund Chen Zhicai
Sport: Tenpin bowling
History: Anson
General Knowledge: Yemen

Nature: Forest that has grown back after being cleared
Money and Power: Asian financial crisis
Language: Central Provident Fund

Quiz 91
Arts and Literature: Postage stamps
Food and Drink: *Mee rebus*
Geography: Boon Keng
Pop Culture: Pierre Png
Sport: 1978
History: Malay State Guides
General Knowledge: Sakya Muni Buddha Gaya Temple
Nature: By diving into the water
Money and Power: SembCorp Industries
Language: Words that sound the same but have different meanings

Quiz 92
Arts and Literature: N. Palanivelu
Food and Drink: Turmeric
Geography: Ecuador
Pop Culture: *Romeo and Juliet*
Sport: 1984
History: Tan Tock Seng Hospital
General Knowledge: Salvation Army
Nature: In burrows in the river bank
Money and Power: Senoko Power
Language: Simplified Chinese

Quiz 93
Arts and Literature: Calligraphy
Food and Drink: Mutton
Geography: Borneo
Pop Culture: Aileen Tan
Sport: Football
History: Hong Kong
General Knowledge: Scouts
Nature: Yellow
Money and Power: Shangri-La
Language: Guobiao code (GB)

Quiz 94
Arts and Literature: A style of Malay poetry

Food and Drink: Biryani
Geography: Great World City
Pop Culture: *The Greatest Love of All*
Sport: FC Basel
History: Medicine
General Knowledge: Tan Tock Seng Hospital
Nature: While it is flying
Money and Power: Raffles Place
Language: Mandarin Chinese

Quiz 95

Arts and Literature: Sriwana
Food and Drink: Vegetarian Society
Geography: Cuscaden Road
Pop Culture: Merlion
Sport: Steve Darby
History: War crimes trials of the Japanese
General Knowledge: Three quarters full
Nature: Peregrine Falcon
Money and Power: United Nations Security Council
Language: Code switching

Quiz 96

Arts and Literature: Photographic Society of Singapore
Food and Drink: Green
Geography: Bukit Panjang
Pop Culture: The Flying Dutchman
Sport: Lim Tong Hai
History: Teochew and Hokkien
General Knowledge: 1987
Nature: They build their nests on vertical surfaces
Money and Power: SilkAir
Language: Austronesian

Quiz 97

Arts and Literature: Phoon Yew Tien
Food and Drink: *Bubur cha cha*
Geography: Changi Village
Pop Culture: *Nokia Football Crazy*
Sport: Nigeria
History: Singapore Police Force
General Knowledge: Hindi

Nature: In the forest canopy
Money and Power: Creative Technology
Language: Malay

Quiz 98
Arts and Literature: Photography
Food and Drink: *Ah balling*
Geography: Pasir Ris Park
Pop Culture: Jean Danker
Sport: Noh Alam Shah
History: Trolley-buses
General Knowledge: Punjab
Nature: A bird
Money and Power: Singapore Airlines
Language: Portuguese

Quiz 99
Arts and Literature: Rudyard Kipling
Food and Drink: Underground
Geography: Sengkang
Pop Culture: Kelvin Tan
Sport: Tao Li
History: Car
General Knowledge: Star of Temasek
Nature: Tent Spider
Money and Power: Cambridge
Language: Vomiting

Celebrity Quiz—Simone Heng
Arts and Literature: Practice Performing Arts School
Food and Drink: Sugar cane
Geography: East Coast Park
Pop Culture: Jade Seah
Sport: 8–0
History: Sinkheh
General Knowledge: Urban Redevelopment Authority (URA)
Nature: Tail feathers
Money and Power: Chee Soon Juan
Language: Tamil
Celebrity Bonus Question: Simone Heng

Quiz 101

Arts and Literature: Architecture
Food and Drink: Long Beach Seafood Restaurant
Geography: Bandar Bintan Telani
Pop Culture: Chen Shucheng
Sport: Theresa Goh
History: Armenians
General Knowledge: Area Licensing Scheme
Nature: Asian Elephant
Money and Power: The Association of Banks in Singapore (ABS)
Language: Baba Malay

Quiz 102

Arts and Literature: Chinese theatre
Food and Drink: Sap
Geography: Orange Grove Road
Pop Culture: Brazil
Sport: Geylang United
History: People's Action Party
General Knowledge: Field gun
Nature: It has a black bill
Money and Power: C. V. Devan Nair
Language: Hokkien

Quiz 103

Arts and Literature: Sarkasi Said
Food and Drink: *Ghee*
Geography: Sim Lim Square
Pop Culture: Hady Mirza
Sport: Selangor
History: Chiang Kai Shek International Airport, Taipei
General Knowledge: Singapore General Hospital (SGH)
Nature: Insects
Money and Power: 1999
Language: *Kamus Dewan*

Quiz 104

Arts and Literature: Sculpture Square
Food and Drink: Congee
Geography: Scotts Road
Pop Culture: Poker
Sport: Lions

History: It was hijacked
General Knowledge: Teutonia Club
Nature: Black and white
Money and Power: Singapore Petroleum Company
Language: Malay

Quiz 105

Arts and Literature: Ink painting
Food and Drink: Peranakan
Geography: Kampong Selak Kain (Pull-Up-Your-Sarong Village)
Pop Culture: Ava Gardner
Sport: Silat
History: Coolie
General Knowledge: City Harvest Church
Nature: Silk
Money and Power: Consumer Association of Singapore (CASE)
Language: Portuguese

Quiz 106

Arts and Literature: Piano
Food and Drink: Liver
Geography: Plaza Singapura
Pop Culture: Lee Tok Kong
Sport: 2003
History: Srivijaya
General Knowledge: The Singapore Stone
Nature: Singing
Money and Power: The Speaker
Language: Sri Lanka

Quiz 107

Arts and Literature: Haresh Sharma
Food and Drink: Mango
Geography: Corporation Road
Pop Culture: Mandopop
Sport: Dolphin
History: Labuan
General Knowledge: Cavenagh Bridge
Nature: It 'sews' large leaves together to cover it
Money and Power: Standards, Productivity and Innovation for Growth (SPRING)
Language: Vattaluttu

Quiz 108

Arts and Literature: Rex Shelley
Food and Drink: Mint
Geography: Kallang River
Pop Culture: The Pump Room
Sport: Jurong West Stadium
History: Calcutta
General Knowledge: Singapore Zoo (she's an orang utan)
Nature: Rainforest
Money and Power: StarHub
Language: Tamil

Quiz 109

Arts and Literature: *Berita Harian*
Food and Drink: Stir-frying
Geography: Fountain of Wealth
Pop Culture: Party
Sport: The Warriors
History: Two
General Knowledge: Tank
Nature: Fly
Money and Power: Ensure that there are a minimum of three opposition MPs in parliament
Language: A closed (yes or no) question

Quiz 110

Arts and Literature: Teochew
Food and Drink: Monosodium glutamate
Geography: Area
Pop Culture: Bernard Lim
Sport: None are originally from Singapore
History: Shooting
General Knowledge: Slavery
Nature: Grassland
Money and Power: Housing & Development Board (HDB)
Language: Tolkappiyam

Quiz 111

Arts and Literature: Singapore Arts Festival
Food and Drink: Green tea
Geography: Airport
Pop Culture: Civil Defence

Sport: Dragon
History: Syed Ja'afar
General Knowledge: Smoking
Nature: Red
Money and Power: Statutory board
Language: Cash

Quiz 112
Arts and Literature: Lee Tzu Pheng
Food and Drink: Steaming
Geography: Geylang
Pop Culture: Taiwan
Sport: An artificial surface
History: Operation Matador
General Knowledge: Omar Kampung Melaka Mosque
Nature: Mangroves
Money and Power: Medisave
Language: J

Celebrity Quiz—Ong Kim Seng
Arts and Literature: Neoclassical
Food and Drink: Chilli crab
Geography: Bawean
Pop Culture: Chew Chor Meng
Sport: Golf
History: 1967
General Knowledge: Black and whites
Nature: Banded leaf monkey
Money and Power: Aw Boon Haw
Language: Hokkien
Celebrity Bonus Question: Javier Perez de Cuellar and Kofi Annan

Quiz 114
Arts and Literature: Singapore Art Museum
Food and Drink: *Bao*
Geography: Population
Pop Culture: Mambo Jambo
Sport: Ram
History: Tan Tock Seng Hospital
General Knowledge: Sri Mariamman Temple
Nature: Nectar
Money and Power: Syariah Court

Language: Catamaran

Quiz 115
Arts and Literature: Chinese opera
Food and Drink: Rosewater
Geography: Kranji Reservoir
Pop Culture: *True Files*
Sport: Redhill Rangers
History: Sun Yat Sen
General Knowledge: Siong Lim Temple (Lian Shan Shuang Lin Monastery)
Nature: East Asia
Money and Power: Standard Chartered Bank
Language: Tamil

Quiz 116
Arts and Literature: Singapore Biennale
Food and Drink: *Bakkwa*
Geography: Area
Pop Culture: Ministry of Sound
Sport: AFC Cup
History: Meter
General Knowledge: Two (Presidents Yusof Ishak and Benjamin Sheares)
Nature: It is the smallest bird in Southeast Asia
Money and Power: Ministry of Finance
Language: Cleavage

Quiz 117
Arts and Literature: Singapore Chinese Orchestra
Food and Drink: Lemongrass
Geography: Population
Pop Culture: *The Fifth Element*
Sport: Douglas Moore
History: 1963
General Knowledge: Lion and tiger
Nature: Rainforest
Money and Power: Temasek Holdings
Language: 'Take you go market and sell'

Quiz 118
Arts and Literature: Singapore Dance Theatre

Food and Drink: Brown
Geography: Singapore Island
Pop Culture: A comic
Sport: Balestier Central
History: 1974
General Knowledge: Vertical marathon
Nature: Sungei Buloh Wetland Reserve
Money and Power: Six
Language: Kwai Lan Kia (troublemaking child)

Quiz 119
Arts and Literature: Nanyang Academy of Fine Arts (NAFA)
Food and Drink: Australia
Geography: Bukit Panjang
Pop Culture: Xinyao
Sport: Sailing
History: Gordon Bennett
General Knowledge: 1967
Nature: At night
Money and Power: E. W. Barker
Language: Mandarin Chinese

Quiz 120
Arts and Literature: Nadiputra
Food and Drink: Lassi
Geography: New Bridge Street
Pop Culture: Mo Jing Jing
Sport: Three
History: Robinsons
General Knowledge: Red Cross
Nature: A bird
Money and Power: A political party
Language: Indo-European

Quiz 121
Arts and Literature: Singapore Lyric Opera
Food and Drink: Thosai
Geography: Straits of Singapore
Pop Culture: The Usual Suspects
Sport: Robert Alberts
History: Tin
General Knowledge: Spikes attached to the devotee's own flesh

Nature: A mammal
Money and Power: QuickPck
Language: Mat

Quiz 122

Arts and Literature: Equator Art Society
Food and Drink: *Tang yuan*
Geography: Clarke Quay
Pop Culture: Tanya Chua
Sport: 100 metres
History: Boys' Brigade
General Knowledge: Bomb shelter
Nature: Two
Money and Power: Law
Language: English

Quiz 123

Arts and Literature: Paper
Food and Drink: Oyster omelette
Geography: MacPherson Road
Pop Culture: Songs of the Sea
Sport: Twenty points
History: Netherlands
General Knowledge: Thian Hock Keng Temple
Nature: SARS
Money and Power: Ten years
Language: Nipples

Quiz 124

Arts and Literature: The Artists' Village
Food and Drink: *Yusheng*
Geography: Bugis Street
Pop Culture: Cabaret
Sport: Singapore Island Country Club
History: Brunei
General Knowledge: Cathay Building
Nature: Chek Jawa
Money and Power: Oversea-Chinese Banking Corporation (OCBC)
Language: Roman script

Quiz 125

Arts and Literature: Chinese opera

Food and Drink: Durian fruit
Geography: Causeway Point
Pop Culture: Class 95FM
Sport: Nazri Nasir
History: Shophouse
General Knowledge: Human faeces
Nature: Mud
Money and Power: Sim Lim Square
Language: By radical

Quiz 126
Arts and Literature: Storytelling
Food and Drink: July
Geography: Via a tunnel
Pop Culture: Siloso Beach
Sport: Raddy Avramovic
History: Water
General Knowledge: Machine Gun
Nature: Asian Koel
Money and Power: United Overseas Bank (UOB)
Language: Chinese

Quiz 127
Arts and Literature: The Substation
Food and Drink: No. 5
Geography: Bishan Park
Pop Culture: Night Safari
Sport: Shebby Singh
History: Rickshaw
General Knowledge: Three (NUS, NTU and SMU)
Nature: A bird
Money and Power: Free Trade Agreement
Language: Japanese

Celebrity Quiz—Chandran Nair
Arts and Literature: Syair
Food and Drink: Mangosteen
Geography: Commonwealth
Pop Culture: CHIJMES
Sport: Netball
History: Postage stamp
General Knowledge: Vesak Day

Nature: A bird
Money and Power: *Wakaf*
Language: 'Obiang'
Celebrity Bonus Question: *Grandfather*

Quiz 129
Arts and Literature: Poetry
Food and Drink: White
Geography: Kembangan
Pop Culture: An observation wheel
Sport: London would host the 2012 Olympic Games
History: Sir William Goode
General Knowledge: Void deck
Nature: Mimicking the human voice
Money and Power: Want Want Holdings
Language: Naval Diving Unit

Quiz 130
Arts and Literature: Tan Chan Boon
Food and Drink: They contain a poisonous substance
Geography: Admiralty
Pop Culture: Golden Mile Complex
Sport: Bodybuilding
History: Temasek
General Knowledge: Property
Nature: Baya Weaver
Money and Power: Journalism
Language: Singapore Armed Forces Reservists' Association

Quiz 131
Arts and Literature: Tan Hwee Hwee
Food and Drink: Dragon fruit
Geography: West coast
Pop Culture: Lucky Plaza
Sport: Swim the English Channel
History: Zheng He
General Knowledge: Plastic surgery
Nature: It has a small backward-pointing 'horn' on its head
Money and Power: Albert Winsemius
Language: Republic of Singapore Air Force

Quiz 132
Arts and Literature: National Arts Council
Food and Drink: Hokkien
Geography: Sembawang
Pop Culture: *The Peak*
Sport: South Korea
History: Dutch
General Knowledge: Republic of Singapore Air Force
Nature: Brown and black
Money and Power: Public Service Commission
Language: English (*Oxford English Dictionary* 2005)

Quiz 133
Arts and Literature: Vanessa Mae
Food and Drink: *Krupuk*
Geography: Pasir Ris Park
Pop Culture: Junction 8
Sport: Nine
History: *The Straits Times*
General Knowledge: Five (Singapore, Temasek, Nanyang, Ngee Ann and Republic)
Nature: The scales reflect the colours of a rainbow
Money and Power: World Trade Organisation
Language: Army Training and Evaluation Centre

Quiz 134
Arts and Literature: Paul Theroux
Food and Drink: Papaya
Geography: Sumatra
Pop Culture: Mustafa Centre
Sport: Instep
History: Singapore Polytechnic
General Knowledge: Marina Bay Floating Stadium
Nature: Lesser Mousedeer
Money and Power: Workforce Development Agency
Language: Walk Around, Look Important

Quiz 135
Arts and Literature: The Arts Fission Company
Food and Drink: *Yum cha*
Geography: Bukit Batok
Pop Culture: Ballads

Sport: Keppel Club
History: 2003
General Knowledge: Golden Mile Complex
Nature: Gecko
Money and Power: United Overseas Bank (UOB)
Language: Nanyang University

Quiz 136

Arts and Literature: Ovidia Yu
Food and Drink: Flower
Geography: Maldives
Pop Culture: White Sands
Sport: 2002
History: 1968
General Knowledge: 2011
Nature: A bat
Money and Power: 'First-past-the-post' system
Language: Basic Combat Training Centre

Quiz 137

Arts and Literature: The Arts House
Food and Drink: Street lighting
Geography: Blood
Pop Culture: Henry Foo (Fu Su Yin)
Sport: Golf
History: Battle of Bukit Timah
General Knowledge: Singapore's tallest building
Nature: Insects
Money and Power: Banyan Tree
Language: English

Quiz 138

Arts and Literature: Arts Theatre of Singapore
Food and Drink: Coffee shop
Geography: There is no 'hill'—it was cleared for redevelopment.
Pop Culture: *The Early Bird Show*
Sport: Jesmine Ho
History: Malay Regiment
General Knowledge: 280 metres
Money and Power: Barisan Socialis
Language: English

Quiz 139
Arts and Literature: Singapore Indian Fine Arts Society
Food and Drink: Jackfruit
Geography: Pulau Serangoon
Pop Culture: Wu Cheng Yi
Sport: Tiong Bahru United
History: Teochew
General Knowledge: One kilometre
Nature: Malaysian Porcupine
Money and Power: Twenty-three
Language: Dubdew

Quiz 140
Arts and Literature: 1930s
Food and Drink: Peranakan
Geography: Zhenghua Town
Pop Culture: Chingay
Sport: Athletics
History: Cathedral of the Good Shepherd
General Knowledge: Automobile Association of Singapore (AAS)
Nature: East Coast
Money and Power: Biopolis
Language: Tamil-speaking Muslims

Quiz 141
Arts and Literature: Nanyang School
Food and Drink: Cairnhill Hotel
Geography: Mount Faber and Sentosa
Pop Culture: Annabel Chong
Sport: Table tennis
History: Black and white houses
General Knowledge: Axe Brand Universal Oil
Nature: 35.8 °C
Money and Power: BNP Paribas
Language: Disaster Assistance & Rescue Team

Quiz 142
Arts and Literature: Chan Yoong Han
Food and Drink: Ice kachang
Geography: Bukit Gombak
Pop Culture: Pony Canyon
Sport: Vincent Ng

History: Changi Prison
General Knowledge: Airbus A380
Nature: Its dorsal spines
Money and Power: Chief Justice
Language: Phua Chu Kang

Quiz 143

Arts and Literature: 1949
Food and Drink: Delifrance
Geography: Christmas Island
Pop Culture: *Richu* (*Sunrise*)
Sport: Judo
History: Subhas Chandra Bose
General Knowledge: Bird flu
Nature: Monsoon
Money and Power: BP
Language: 'Onward Singapore'

Quiz 144

Arts and Literature: Catherine Lim
Food and Drink: Salak
Geography: Ang Mo Kio
Pop Culture: Taufik Batisah
Sport: Hockey
History: 1915
General Knowledge: Underground ammunition bunkers
Nature: Birds
Money and Power: 1967
Language: A term to describe something very good (a translation of the Hokkien expression '*bo bei chow*' used in horse-racing jargon to describe a champion horse which is way ahead of the field)

Quiz 145

Arts and Literature: Singapore Repertory Theatre
Food and Drink: Chilli crab
Geography: Length of coastline
Pop Culture: Carlsberg Sky Tower
Sport: Egmar Goncalves
History: United Nations
General Knowledge: Fire-walking
Nature: Poison
Money and Power: Member of Parliament (MP)

Language: No Action, Talk Only

Quiz 146
Arts and Literature: Modern art
Food and Drink: One month
Geography: Clifford Pier
Pop Culture: Cinema on wheels
Sport: Li Jiawei
History: Britannia Club
General Knowledge: Boys' Brigade
Nature: King Cobra
Money and Power: S$1,000
Language: Small- or Medium-sized Enterprise

Quiz 147
Arts and Literature: Tang Da Wu
Food and Drink: Devil's curry
Geography: One
Pop Culture: Concave Scream
Sport: Badminton
History: 1936
General Knowledge: Forty
Nature: Black Spitting Cobra
Money and Power: CapitaLand
Language: Economic Development Board

Quiz 148
Arts and Literature: Trimurti
Food and Drink: Smore
Geography: Chinatown
Pop Culture: Babes Conde
Sport: Squash
History: British Military Administration (BMA)
General Knowledge: Buddhism
Nature: Land reclamation
Money and Power: Real Estate Investment Trust (REIT)
Language: Monetary Authority of Singapore

Quiz 149
Arts and Literature: 1976
Food and Drink: Brandy
Geography: Sea wall

Pop Culture: The Crescendos
Sport: Malaysia Cup
History: 1971
General Knowledge: A cemetery
Nature: March to April
Money and Power: Casino ship
Language: Group Representation Constituency

Quiz 150

Arts and Literature: ASEAN Sculpture Garden
Food and Drink: Snapper
Geography: Dempsey Road
Pop Culture: *Eating Air*
Sport: 1967
History: Bukit Ho Swee
General Knowledge: Rattan
Nature: Mosaic Crab
Money and Power: Central Provident Fund (CPF)
Language: Electronic Road Pricing

Celebrity Quiz—Sir Stamford Raffles

Arts and Literature: ASAS 50
Food and Drink: Toman fish
Geography: Deep Tunnel Sewerage System
Pop Culture: Wilson David
Sport: Twenty-two
History: Bugis
General Knowledge: Mount Faber
Nature: Crown-of-thorns Starfish
Money and Power: 1973
Language: Single Member Constituency
Celebrity Bonus Question: Botany

Quiz 152

Arts and Literature: 1955
Food and Drink: Sugar
Geography: Boon Lay
Pop Culture: Billy Koh
Sport: Singapore Turf Club
History: Income tax
General Knowledge: Suntec City
Nature: Flying Fox

Money and Power: People's Action Party (PAP)
Language: Brunei

Quiz 153
Arts and Literature: Musical
Food and Drink: Scotts Picnic Food Court
Geography: Orchard Road
Pop Culture: Crazy Horse
Sport: Mardan Mamat
History: Cable car disaster
General Knowledge: Catholicism
Nature: Sungei Buloh Wetland Reserve
Money and Power: Chan Sek Keong
Language: Standard Singapore(an) English

Quiz 154
Arts and Literature: Batik
Food and Drink: Food Republic
Geography: Endau
Pop Culture: Cliff Richard and the Shadows
Sport: Hockey
History: Stop at Two Campaign
General Knowledge: Fallen British soldiers from World Wars I and II
Nature: Household food waste
Money and Power: Chartered Semiconductors
Language: Standard Singapore(an) English (SSE)

Quiz 155
Arts and Literature: Anthony Burgess
Food and Drink: Durian
Geography: Arab Street
Pop Culture: Happy World
Sport: Azman Abdullah
History: The $10 note carried an illustration of a banana tree
General Knowledge: Acupuncture
Nature: Birds
Money and Power: Ten
Language: Backwards (the pidgin English expression originates from the nautical phrase 'go astern')

Quiz 156
Arts and Literature: The floor

Food and Drink: 1932
Geography: East Coast Parkway (ECP)
Pop Culture: *Pop Inn*
Sport: 50,000
History: Electronic Road Pricing (ERP)
General Knowledge: Fifteen years
Nature: Trees
Money and Power: Chee Soon Juan
Language: Singlish

Quiz 157
Arts and Literature: Leslie Charteris
Food and Drink: Biscuits
Geography: Geylang Serai
Pop Culture: Odyssey Music
Sport: 110 metres hurdles
History: Chin Peng
General Knowledge: Four (Terminal 1, Terminal 2, Terminal 3 and Budget Terminal)
Nature: It inflates its body
Money and Power: Chief of Defence Force
Language: Speak Good English Movement

Quiz 158
Arts and Literature: India and Thailand
Food and Drink: Harry's Bar
Geography: Fort Siloso
Pop Culture: 'Yellow' culture
Sport: Southeast Asian Games
History: His leg
General Knowledge: Central Sikh Temple
Nature: Water
Money and Power: Embezzlement
Language: Hokkien

Quiz 159
Arts and Literature: *The Singapore Story*
Food and Drink: Hawker centres
Geography: Sedimentary rock
Pop Culture: Tokyo Square
Sport: National Stadium
History: Census

General Knowledge: Eight years
Nature: During the Japanese Occupation (1942–45)
Money and Power: Chia Thye Poh
Language: Schools

Quiz 160

Arts and Literature: Dennis Bloodworth
Food and Drink: *Hokkien mee*
Geography: Igneous rock
Pop Culture: *BigO*
Sport: Kallang roar
History: Japan
General Knowledge: The highest unsuccessful bid price plus S$1
Nature: Seahorse
Money and Power: Potong Pasir
Language: Four (English, Malay, Mandarin Chinese and Tamil)

Quiz 161

Arts and Literature: Bali
Food and Drink: To stop the gravy running out
Geography: Straits of Johor
Pop Culture: Chongay Organisation
Sport: Khoo Swee Chiow
History: Borneo Company
General Knowledge: Armoured personnel carrier
Nature: 19.4 °C
Money and Power: Borneo Motors
Language: Distinguished Service Order

Quiz 162

Arts and Literature: Classical Indian dance
Food and Drink: Hakka
Geography: Swamp
Pop Culture: The Crescendos
Sport: 1973
History: Certificate of Entitlement (COE)
General Knowledge: Department of Statistics (DOS)
Nature: Bukit Timah Nature Reserve
Money and Power: Jurong Island
Language: Bazaar Malay

Quiz 163

Arts and Literature: Paul Abisheganaden
Food and Drink: Peranakan
Geography: 162 metres
Pop Culture: Esplanade – Theatres on the Bay
Sport: Ronald Susilo
History: Chinese middle school riots
General Knowledge: Chao Tzee Cheng
Nature: Human remains
Money and Power: Chin Peng
Language: Housing Development Board

Quiz 164

Arts and Literature: Watercolour
Food and Drink: Les Amis
Geography: Pulau Tekong
Pop Culture: *Blessings*
Sport: Shooting
History: Chinese New Year
General Knowledge: Mathematics
Nature: Soon Hock
Money and Power: China Aviation Oil
Language: Urban Redevelopment Authority

Quiz 165

Arts and Literature: *Lat Pau*
Food and Drink: Curry puff
Geography: Katong
Pop Culture: *Saint Jack*
Sport: Singapore Badminton Hall
History: Obelisk
General Knowledge: Condominium
Nature: A bird dropping
Money and Power: Singapore Island Country Club
Language: 'Good morning'

Quiz 166

Arts and Literature: Gopal Baratham
Food and Drink: Naan
Geography: Cambodia
Pop Culture: 'Best in Singapore and JB, and some say Batam.'
Sport: Balestier Road

History: The first airplane take-off in Singapore
General Knowledge: Michael Fay
Nature: One third
Money and Power: Dr Vivian Balakrishnan
Language: Alliance Française

Quiz 167
Arts and Literature: *The Man in the Cupboard*
Food and Drink: Milk bars
Geography: Hougang
Pop Culture: Astreal
Sport: Badminton
History: Protestantism
General Knowledge: Zao Chen (the Kitchen God)
Nature: GloFish
Money and Power: Chua Kim Yeow
Language: Tampines Expressway

Quiz 168
Arts and Literature: Radio
Food and Drink: Coconut milk
Geography: Sixty-three
Pop Culture: Fann Wong
Sport: Ouzo
History: Map
General Knowledge: Nian
Nature: The water is not polluted
Money and Power: Citigroup
Language: Convent of the Holy Infant Jesus

Quiz 169
Arts and Literature: Musical instruments
Food and Drink: NEWater
Geography: Pulau Brani
Pop Culture: *15*
Sport: Cricket
History: Comfort women
General Knowledge: Hongbao
Nature: Heritage trees
Money and Power: Citizens' Consultative Committee (CCC)
Language: Development Bank of Singapore

Quiz 170
Arts and Literature: Chinese classical music
Food and Drink: Newton Food Centre
Geography: Jinricksha Station
Pop Culture: Empire
Sport: Hockey
History: 1965
General Knowledge: Shen
Nature: HSBC TreeTop Walk
Money and Power: City Council
Language: Port of Singapore Authority

Quiz 171
Arts and Literature: 1986
Food and Drink: Sir Stamford Raffles
Geography: Jurong
Pop Culture: It was Singapore's first colour film production
Sport: Three
History: Confrontasion (Konfrontasi)
General Knowledge: Armenian Church
Nature: They rub their body parts together
Money and Power: Civil Service College (CSC)
Language: Jurong Town Corporation

Celebrity Quiz—Khoo Swee Chiow
Arts and Literature: Chinese zither
Food and Drink: FairPrice
Geography: Johor Bahru
Pop Culture: *Laila Majnun*
Sport: Three
History: Comprador
General Knowledge: Feng Shui
Nature: Cicada
Money and Power: City Developments Limited (CDL)
Language: Network for Electronic Transfers
Celebrity Bonus Question: Inline Skating

Quiz 173
Arts and Literature: People's Association Chinese Orchestra
Food and Drink: Nutmeg
Geography: Jurong Island
Pop Culture: Malay

Sport: Hand
History: Confucius
General Knowledge: Christmas tree
Nature: Praying mantis
Money and Power: Clerk of Parliament
Language: Handphone

Quiz 174

Arts and Literature: *Xin Guomin Ribao* (*New Citizen Daily*)
Food and Drink: Popiah
Geography: Keppel Harbour
Pop Culture: *Forever Fever*
Sport: Singapore Cricket Club
History: Double tenth incident
General Knowledge: Confucianism
Nature: They warn predators that it doesn't taste good
Money and Power: Court of Appeal
Language: 'Wind and water'

Quiz 175

Arts and Literature: Pro-communist political songs from mainland China
Food and Drink: Gambier
Geography: Kampong
Pop Culture: Bing Crosby and Bob Hope
Sport: A Malay martial art
History: Flor Contemplacion
General Knowledge: Singaporean citizenship
Nature: Black Crazy Ant
Money and Power: Association of Southeast Asian Nations (ASEAN)
Language: Kristang

Quiz 176

Arts and Literature: Lynette Seah
Food and Drink: Claypot cooking
Geography: Raffles City
Pop Culture: Huang Biren
Sport: Red
History: Sri Mariamman Temple
General Knowledge: Anglo-Chinese School
Nature: A bird
Money and Power: Singapore Press Holdings (SPH)

Language: Dravidian

Quiz 177
Arts and Literature: Abdul Ghani Abdul Hamid
Food and Drink: Iced Horlicks with an extra scoop of Horlicks powder on top
Geography: Bishan
Pop Culture: Before I Get Old
Sport: Chee Swee Lee
History: Divide it between themselves
General Knowledge: Alhambra
Nature: Forest
Money and Power: Opthalmology
Language: Asia-Pacific Economic Cooperation

Quiz 178
Arts and Literature: Calligraphy
Food and Drink: Pineapples
Geography: Kampong
Pop Culture: *Rogue Trader*
Sport: Sailing
History: Dalforce
General Knowledge: Red beret
Nature: 2.5 centimetres
Money and Power: Fraser & Neave
Language: 'Have you eaten?'

Quiz 179
Arts and Literature: Chen Wen Hsi
Food and Drink: Red
Geography: Horsbrugh Lighthouse
Pop Culture: Humpback Oak
Sport: Remy Ong
History: Chinese Protectorate
General Knowledge: Chewing gum
Nature: Plankton
Money and Power: 1990
Language: Singapore Mass Rapid Transit

Quiz 180
Arts and Literature: City Chinese Orchestra
Food and Drink: Curry puff

Geography: Kampong Glam
Pop Culture: *The Letter*
Sport: 1990
History: Constitution
General Knowledge: Church of St Joseph
Nature: Fungus
Money and Power: Colonial Office
Language: Retrenchment

Quiz 181
Arts and Literature: *Huang Dao* (*Deserted Island*)
Food and Drink: Red House Bakery
Geography: Kreta Ayer
Pop Culture: Great World
Sport: Singapore Grand Prix
History: Bencoolen
General Knowledge: Daching
Nature: Common Tree Nymph
Money and Power: Creative Technology
Language: Foochow

Quiz 182
Arts and Literature: Nanyang Chinese literature
Food and Drink: *Rojak*
Geography: Kusu Island
Pop Culture: Cathay-Keris Films
Sport: Velodrome
History: Hong Kong
General Knowledge: New converts to Islam
Nature: Common Birdwing
Money and Power: 1967
Language: Severe Acute Respiratory Syndrome

Quiz 183
Arts and Literature: Singapore Chinese literature
Food and Drink: French loaf
Geography: 15 metres
Pop Culture: P. Ramlee
Sport: Four
History: Emergency
General Knowledge: Sewer water
Nature: Stick insect

Money and Power: Economic Development Board (EDB)
Language: Gross Domestic Product

Quiz 184
Arts and Literature: Alex Abisheganaden
Food and Drink: The Carnation brand of evaporated milk
Geography: Negri Sembilan
Pop Culture: Bhumiband
Sport: Simon Chua
History: United Malays National Organisation (UMNO)
General Knowledge: Armenian Church
Nature: White-vented or Javan Myna
Money and Power: E.W. Barker
Language: Jawi

Quiz 185
Arts and Literature: 1995
Food and Drink: Chennai (Madras)
Geography: Land area
Pop Culture: *Her World*
Sport: Sikh
History: Faber House
General Knowledge: Baby Bonus Scheme
Nature: Labrador Nature Reserve
Money and Power: Military
Language: Hong Kong & Shanghai Banking Corporation

Quiz 186
Arts and Literature: *Mulian Jiu Mu* (*Mulian Rescues His Mother From Hell*)
Food and Drink: Winter melon
Geography: MacRitchie Reservoir
Pop Culture: *I Not Stupid*
Sport: Swimming
History: Ford Motor Factory
General Knowledge: Hari Raya Haji (Eid-ul-Adha)
Nature: Liana
Money and Power: Monetary Authority of Singapore (MAS)
Language: *Lat Pau*

Quiz 187
Arts and Literature: Street

Food and Drink: Tea halia
Geography: Monaco
Pop Culture: Huang Wenyang
Sport: Singapore Recreation Club
History: Colonel William Farquhar
General Knowledge: Dragon boat races
Nature: Horseshoe Crab
Money and Power: Economic Development Board (EDB)
Language: Jawi

Quiz 188
Arts and Literature: Munshi Abdullah
Food and Drink: Milo (Nestlé Milo often uses football as the theme of its advertisements)
Geography: Ang Mo Kio
Pop Culture: Bar-top dancing
Sport: Swimming
History: Abdul Rahman
General Knowledge: Anglo-Chinese School
Nature: Forest
Money and Power: Kwong Yik Bank
Language: Association of Women for Action and Research

Quiz 189
Arts and Literature: They celebrate a religious event
Food and Drink: Peanut
Geography: Little India
Pop Culture: Hussain Haniff
Sport: Singapore Sevens
History: Michael Fay
General Knowledge: Early Founders' Memorial Stone
Nature: Painkillers
Money and Power: Entrepôt
Language: Land Transport Authority

Quiz 190
Arts and Literature: Chinese opera
Food and Drink: Sarabat stalls
Geography: Shenton Way
Pop Culture: Sun (Ho Yeow Sun)
Sport: Singapore Pools
History: Fajar trial

General Knowledge: Dengue fever
Nature: Fern
Money and Power: East Asia Summit (EAS)
Language: National Registration Identity Card

Quiz 191
Arts and Literature: Chinatown
Food and Drink: Singapore Sling
Geography: Pulau Ubin
Pop Culture: Ashley Isham
Sport: They are inducted into the Hall of Fame
History: 1824
General Knowledge: Hari Raya Puasa (Eid-ul-Fitr)
Nature: Mammal
Money and Power: 40%
Language: *Lianhe Zaobao*

Quiz 192
Arts and Literature: Chinese Theatre Circle
Food and Drink: Vodka
Geography: Marina Barrage
Pop Culture: Jiang Hu
Sport: Singapore Sports School (SSS)
History: Singapore Post Office
General Knowledge: Sir Stamford Raffles
Nature: Tiger
Money and Power: Edusave
Language: Malay

Quiz 193
Arts and Literature: Chng Seok Tin
Food and Drink: Cabbage
Geography: North East Line
Pop Culture: Drive-in cinema
Sport: Singapore Swimming Club
History: General election
General Knowledge: 2002
Nature: Bat
Money and Power: ElderShield
Language: Johor-Riau

Quiz 194

Arts and Literature: Bangsawan
Food and Drink: Fitzpatrick's
Geography: Dhoby Ghaut
Pop Culture: Electrico
Sport: Pahang
History: Electric trams
General Knowledge: Certificate of Entitlement (COE)
Nature: Crab
Money and Power: 2.5%
Language: Sylvia Toh Paik Choo

Celebrity Quiz—Suchen Christine Lim

Arts and Literature: They were suspected of left-wing political activity
Food and Drink: Marrow and cartilage
Geography: Nicoll Highway
Pop Culture: Kumar
Sport: Farrer Park
History: Godowns
General Knowledge: Field gun
Nature: Insects
Money and Power: Five years
Language: Bahasa Malaysia
Celebrity Bonus Question: *Fistful of Colours*

Quiz 196

Arts and Literature: Drama Box
Food and Drink: Tee Yih Jia
Geography: Mount Faber
Pop Culture: L. Krishnan
Sport: 2000
History: Goh Chok Tong
General Knowledge: Five feet
Nature: Echolocation
Money and Power: President
Language: *'Sebutan baku'*

Quiz 197

Arts and Literature: Choo Hoey
Food and Drink: Teh tarik
Geography: Nanyang
Pop Culture: Dick Lee

Sport: 1996
History: Gold bar murders
General Knowledge: Flag of convenience
Nature: Black and white
Money and Power: Twenty-one
Language: *Berita Harian*

Quiz 198

Arts and Literature: Ink painting
Food and Drink: Tekka Market
Geography: Upper Seletar Reservoir
Pop Culture: Li Nanxing (Jonathan Li)
Sport: Geylang United
History: Governors
General Knowledge: S$2,500
Nature: Giant squirrel
Money and Power: *Government Gazette*
Language: Suria

Quiz 199

Arts and Literature: Wang Runhua
Food and Drink: *Roti prata*
Geography: They all lie on reclaimed land
Pop Culture: Mavis Hee
Sport: Bukit course
History: Sir Henry Gurney
General Knowledge: Deepavali
Nature: Turtle
Money and Power: Donaldson & Burkinshaw
Language: Hokkien

Quiz 200

Arts and Literature: Photography
Food and Drink: Because they always had wet floors
Geography: Padang
Pop Culture: Li Brothers (Li Sisong and Li Weisong)
Sport: Match-fixing
History: Maria Hertogh
General Knowledge: Work permit
Nature: At night
Money and Power: Elections Department
Language: Majlis Bahasa Melayu Singapura (MBMS) (Malay Language
Council Singapore)